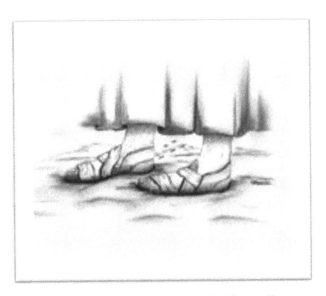

"Walk A Mile in MY Shoes"

Drawn by

Bonnie Lou Oliver

Dedication

✝

This book is dedicated to my Mom and Dad, Columbus and Leanna Oliver, who raised me to grow into a man of Faith; To my Family, To my lovely wife Bonnie who not only stuck by me but fought feverously to obtain justice so that *'walking free'* would become a reality for me: To Barbara my sister-in-law who stuck by Bonnie and I even though the road was long and hard. Most of all to my Lord and Savior who has kept every promise He made to me. Finally, to all those many prayer warriors who took the time to listen to us and prayed for us along the way.

Walking Free

From Bondage to Liberty

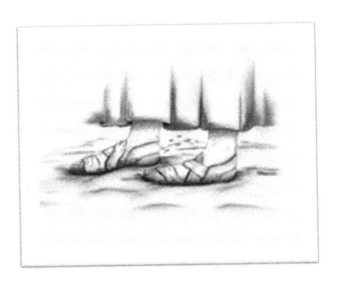

by
Gregory Oliver

With Excerpts by
Bonnie Lou Oliver

To order additional copies of this book, contact:
Proisle publishing Services LLC
1177 6th Ave 5th Floor
New York, NY 10036, USA
Phone: (+1 347-922-3779)
info@proislepublishing.com

PROISLE PUBLISHING

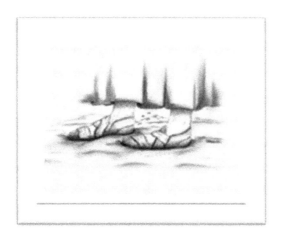

✟

All stories, events and
conversations
are as I remember them.

Walking Free
From Bondage to Liberty

✝

Table of Contents

Acknowledgments

It is to God I live and have my being; I give all thanks and Glory unto the Lord for he brought me out of bondage into his glorious liberty. He saved me and set my feet upon a solid rock and has established my goings. Thanks to a Michigan woman who found her way down to the City Jail in St. Louis. A special thanks goes to her family who help shape her environment so that she did not look down on people because of their differences. She was able to sift through the pretenses around my case and see me for who I really am. When she heard that I was innocent from the staff members she did not shrink back from doing what was right to right a wrong. There are some hard things in life people face. Bonnie is truly a Good Samaritan, and Heavenly rewards await her and those who treat their neighbors as the Lord has commanded them to do.

Preface

✝

I feel moved and humbled by the Lord to be able to share my life's story in hopes that God's work is ever-present in places we think they aren't. Even though it was the worst of times it also was the best of times. When you are locked away in a prison considered to be the worst of the worst. Living in close proximity with over 5000 inmates of all types of attitudes and walks of life it is not always easy to remain positive. It took the Lord to develop within me a *"peace that passes all understanding,"* and to create a love within my heart to love the unlovely even when others did not or could not.

I remember one time the Lord spoke a word to me saying, "Gregory I can love those that you can't," That taught me my love walk had a great deal of construction to undergo, but I knew that with the help of the Holy Spirit the Lord would get me there on time. I think that the Lord's love is so far-reaching that he knew how to help me apply his love towards those who were wounded and hurt. At the same time, He comforted me with His loving-kindness. *"Walking Free"* will help one get into a deeper walk with the Lord and discover his plan like never before.

It takes us yielding and *"trusting in the Lord with all our heart and not leaning on our own understanding and he will direct thy paths."* I think one of God's love gifts to me was when He blessed me with a beautiful helpmate in my wife Bonnie. She proved herself faithful as she went through tremendous trials and hardships yet remaining obedient to what the Lord called her to do.

Introduction

"*Walking Free*" is going to take time to really focus because that is where we are at right now in our society. We must be "*Walking Free*" from all the evils that the enemy has tried to throw at us. Whether it is drugs, illicit sex, the love of money and power, etc... The enemy is trying to destroy the people of God and "*Walking Free*" is a book that is going to help people to understand what is needed for us to be "*Walking Free*" in the twenty-first century. This book is also a story about a man who spent twenty-two years and five days in prison for a crime he did not commit because the state chose to concoct a story and used whatever means they could illegally to get a conviction. Once they had a conviction the merits of the case were never looked at or acted upon. Every appeal resulted in adding more lies to the already concocted story to favor the court and its erroneous verdict.

CHAPTER 1

"Rigged"
by
Gregory & Bonnie

I sat in a small cell that I shared with another inmate. I was feeling uneasy about the reasons behind the living death sentence I received (a living death sentence is a life sentence without parole running wild with a life sentence with parole). Twelve years had already passed of my life sentence. They had convicted me of first-degree murder and first-degree criminal assault. Anything I knew about my case and lack of evidence proved my innocence, not my guilt, yet here I was imprisoned for the rest of my natural life. I was confident, however, that one day my prayers would be answered, and I would soon be *"Walking Free"*.

One day a still small voice deep inside me was causing me to question whether my stand of innocence was in vain or not. I knew, in my heart, that I had not murdered anyone or assaulted anyone either, but something was causing me to inquire of the Lord on this day. "Lord, is there anything I did that is deserving of this punishment? If there is, then please let me know. I am man enough to deal with any wrongs I have done. I need to know so I can repent and move on with my life." I prayed that the Lord would reveal to me anything that I did that deserved lifelong incarceration so I would know what I would have to do to make amends. I was pleading for the truth, but not the kind of truth that would expose the travesties around imprisonment and bring those who wronged me down in vengeance. No, instead I was asking the Lord to reveal any errors I made in my life that would have caused me this hard time that had taken so many good years out of my life already. I was asking so I could deal with whatever the Lord had for me to help me so that I could be a blessing to others...even in prison.

For years, I told anyone who would listen to me that I was not only innocent but that the Lord was going to set me free. During this time of seeking the Lord's guidance, I heard in an almost audible voice from the Lord saying, "*It was rigged!*"

"Rigged?" I challenged the Lord, as a wave of righteous anger rose up inside me. I knew through the years of study that Bonnie (my advocate) and I did, that we had uncovered the necessary evidence that would prove that my trial was unfair and many of my constitutional rights had been grossly violated...but "rigged?" It was from this time of seeking the Lord that I knew He was going to clear my name some way—somehow, but I did not know-how. *How could they have rigged the trial?* I pondered this at length. What would it take for a case or trial to be rigged? There would have to be a dishonest prosecutor who had political ambitions. We had discovered that the DA at the time of my trial was disbarred two years after my conviction. A defense council that went along, and a judge that would be willing to go along with everything. We had that too. The judge knew he was on a slippery slope and knew that they could be in trouble with the statute they tried the case on if the defense council was correct in their objection to the use of the statute 491.074. As we were to learn, through many studies and many divine

2

appointments, there were a lot more players that were involved in spinning the wheels of injustice in my case than we could even imagine and would evidentially discover. We were on the brink of even more breakthroughs on my case? Or would all our years of hard work be in vain? Only God would have the answers to that and any other question we *still* had about my wrongful imprisonment. I continued to have this burning fire in me of righteous indignation to stand against this erroneous conviction no matter what it took or how long it took.

In the beginning, both Bonnie and I trusted the system and could not believe that judges and lawyers would misapply the law to convict someone of something they did not do. But after years of study, both Bonnie and I were troubled over what we were uncovering about the lack of ethics in the courtroom—all that just for the win regardless of what it took. In this case two wins. Convictions for both Ronald and I. Ah, is this what they call being tough on crime for their own record?

I walked out into the prison population with new hope in my heart and a special glow knowing the Lord had once again revealed more truth to me about my case. Yet, I really did not know how we would acquire the knowledge that would expose the truth. This was not something you could go to anyone about to try and expose all the travesties in my case. We needed proof and hard evidence to prove there was misconduct on the part of authorities. So, with all the boldness I could muster up I started professing, as I had so many times, that the Lord had spoken to me and that I was a "gone man and you can't stop a gone man."

Hanging on my cell wall was a slogan I began saying years before my case went up to the governor's office and

Bonnie and I got married, "Out the door in '94." Ten years passed without a gubernatorial decision as my case sat there through three governors. I kept the sign up regardless of what anyone said, which motivated the men to criticize me unmercifully. In my mind and heart, I was a free man and was already *"Walking Free."* I was free of my negative surroundings; free of the humiliation I had suffered from my wrongful incarceration; free of the bad reputation my name now had been a convicted felon, and free from the harassment heaped upon me by the other inmates who didn't believe I was innocent. Instead, other inmates would tell me that I needed to get my "grave clothes" ready because I was going to die in prison. The reality of my situation was hard and clearing my name became paramount to me.

Through all the harassment I took, I maintained a positive attitude with a ready smile for everyone—guards and inmates alike. I never backed down when being mocked, however, and would not compromise what I honestly believed the Lord had said to me. To many of the inmates, my stand of faith was a joke, but to me, it was my life, and it is what gave me the ability to stand tall amid an ugly, angry environment.

I have fought this case through every legal remedy in accordance with the law and I presented it with legal representation when required. Although the law allows you to represent yourself when one chooses to defend himself from wrongs that are stacked against him. This is where your legal representation may not come to that challenge that is before them. I discovered from one of my attorneys that the state was paying stipends to certain defense attorneys. This is a form of a gift and if that is the case it can pervert justice. He was paying his rent with this money and when they took it away from him, he lost his building. It was at this point he was the attorney that was so angry that in his study he realized this was a rigged case based upon a concocted story and they had to do whatever was necessary to protect the erroneous verdict with more lies. Would he have told me this if the state was continuing to pay him a stipend? It appears although I had a piece of the puzzle that it was rigged when he brought in the concocted story the picture became clear of what the state had done, and since then they have not wanted to address the merits. Therefore, I am now presenting my case to the court of public opinion.

> *"Whatever disunites man from God, also disunites man from man."* —Edmond Burke

by
Bonnie

The years passed and I watched Gregory and listened to his stands of faith and even I became weary, tired of his case, tired of his past, and tired of his preaching faith to himself, which really came across as him preaching to me. What I eventually discovered though was that his stance of faith was a meditation on the Word working within himself, which in turn built a fortress of faith that could not be penetrated by the negativity and bombardment of the enemy who tried to destroy his stance of faith. And he was always the one to encourage—never wavering. After years of study, we knew that some of the authorities we finally got to listen to us were beginning to see the truth as we knew it, but they, too, were bound by the law and the legal lies that hid not only Gregory's innocence but the manipulation and misuse of constitutional law.

When we managed to get Gregory's case up to the governor's office in 1994, we thought it was the end of waiting and that justice would finally prevail. Freedom was only months away—then—tragedy hit, and the Missouri governor died in a plane crash. My spirit was crushed a little too, but Gregory never seemed to falter. In three months, there would be a new governor and his staff would also change...what would happen to all our work and Gregory's case.

There was hope though, for Joe Bednar, the Governor's Chief Council, who I had worked closely with. He was the only person from the current administration that was going into the next administration to work on unfinished business that would carry over. Mr. Bednar promised us that he would take Gregory's case into the new administration and inform the new legal counsel of it. The second advantage we had, of course, was the promise the Lord made to Gregory that one day he would be *"Walking Free."*

I always believed Gregory would not have to spend the rest of his life in prison. Those who knew both of us also believed that Gregory would be free one day. They would tell me that they either had a dream or vision of his freedom. The question was never "if" it was always "when" he would walk from prison and be the person that the Lord ordained him to be.

From the time I first met Gregory I knew there was something special about him, but I couldn't put my finger on it. Then one day when we were visiting, I discovered the answer from that small still voice of the Lord. Gregory was talking about a subject he was engrossed in. Suddenly, I could hear his voice, but I was in another world talking to the Lord myself. "Lord?" I asked, "What is it about this man?" As clear as a bell I heard the Lord say, "In the spirit of David, he is a man after my own heart." Just as suddenly I was back to reality giving Gregory my full attention. Months would go by before I told Gregory about that message, I received from the Lord that special day. I think that it was this message that helped to keep me hanging in there and continually trying to convince authorities of Gregory's innocence,

> *"Courage faces fear and thereby masters it. Cowardice represses fear and is thereby mastered by it."* —Dr. Martin Luther King"

> *We build dikes of courage to hold back the flood of fear."* —Dr. Martin Luther King.

CHAPTER 2
The Crime Based on the Transcripts
My Early Study
by
Bonnie

The blue Ford Mustang sped to an abrupt stop on one rain-slick night during the early morning hours of June 7th, 1985. The St. Louis City police officers rushed the car to apprehend its two occupants. The instructions had been—"Shoot to kill!" The passengers of the car created no problems for the officers of the roadblock. Gregory, a tall brown-skinned young man was driving his brother Ronald's car when apprehended.

"Pretty good driving," one of the officers said to Gregory Oliver as the brothers assumed the position. They were frisked and read their rights before being escorted down to City Jail for questioning. Ronald Oliver, Gregory's younger brother, had just tripped out mentally, which resulted in the death of one man and gunshot wounds to two others.

Gregory was questioned as a witness to the crime without the presence of a lawyer. After questioning, Gregory was confused when the police officer said, "Book um!" Both Gregory and Ronald were booked for the same first-degree murder charge, two first-degree criminal assault charges, and initially, both Gregory and Ronald were charged with kid-napping.

At Ronald's arraignment, the judge told Mrs. Oliver, the boy's mother, that there was no evidence against Gregory. At Gregory's arraignment, however, the story was different, and he was shocked when the judge held him over for probable cause. He was even more shocked when the grand jury came back with a "true bill" for the charges.

The Crime

On the morning of June 6, 1985, Gregory received a collect call from an old girlfriend, Diane. She had just gotten out of jail for auto theft and asked if he would pick her up and either take her to get food stamps or to go over to another party's house to borrow some money. Gregory was unable to help her at the time because he had a small moving job to do that day. Gregory called his brother, Ronald, to see if he could give her a ride. Ronald was also unavailable. So, when Diane called collect a second time, Gregory let her know neither he nor Ronald could oblige her.

Gregory went about his business for that day by taking care of the small moving job he had lined up. His car was out of commission, so he called a cousin to help him. When the job was completed, his cousin was not able to take Gregory all the way home; so, Gregory asked to be dropped off where he saw a couple of familiar faces. Elizabeth an old family friend was passing by with her youngest child's father Sammy Lee Fields. They picked Gregory up and took him to Elizabeth's house to play cards. Elizabeth used to go out with Gregory's older half-brother, Charles.

While at Elizabeth's, Gregory called his mother's house to see if one of his brothers could give him a ride home. No one was available at the time, so he stayed at Elizabeth's apartment most of the afternoon playing cards with a couple other friends. Elizabeth and her friends had already been drinking a little. With some of Gregory's winnings, he sent out to get something else to drink. Elizabeth tried to call Gregory's mother again to see if there was anyone available yet to give Gregory a ride. Later Gregory called a third time and found out that his brother Ronald was on his way. When Ronald arrived, no one seemed to be in any hurry to break up the game, so Ronald sat down to observe. (pp. 843-870, 332, 334, 716, 717, 723 [TT] Trial Transcripts)

During the card game, someone suddenly flicked the lights off and on about three times. This excited Ronald and caused him to "trip out." He pulled out a gun and began shooting randomly into the ceiling. He then kicked out the window and told everyone not to move. (pp. 335 TT) Fortunately, no one was hurt during this incident.

Immediately after that, Elizabeth and Ronald went outside and began arguing over the shooting incident. There was a young neighbor boy outside and Ronald started picking on him. Elizabeth insisted that Ronald leave the boy and sent the boy back to his house. Gregory came out and joined them while Elizabeth and Ronald were still arguing with each other. After the argument between Elizabeth and Ronald was over. The three of them got into Ronald's car. (pp. 341, 680, 730 TT)

Ronald, Gregory, and Elizabeth got into the car (The transcripts are not clear at that point as to all of the circumstances around it.) While driving, Ronald began acting up again and held the gun to Elizabeth's ribs. After a heated discussion, Ronald gave the gun to Gregory who was cramped up in the back seat of the car. Gregory began unloading the gun and throwing the shell casings out the window (The shell casings were found by the police where Elizabeth and Gregory's testimony indicated they would be found.) Unbeknown to Gregory while he was unloading the gun, a round was still in the chamber and the gun discharged accidentally making a hole in the inside side panel of Ronald's car. Ronald angered, insisted Gregory give him the gun back. Gregory obliged seeing the gun was empty and was no longer a threat to anyone. Ronald, still angry over the last incident, was arguing with Gregory. Ronald finally said he was going to put the gun away, so he pulled over and got out of the car, moving to the trunk to dispose of the gun. Gregory and Elizabeth also got out Ronald still had the gun. Elizabeth was hiding behind Gregory telling Gregory, "Don't let him shoot me." (pp. 341, 343, 680, 681, 730 TT)

"No, Pee Wee (Ronald's nickname), man, I'm not going to let you shoot Elizabeth," Gregory said.

"If you don't move, I'll shoot you too, brother or not," was Ronald's reply. (pp. 343, 683 TT)

Elizabeth knew for sure that Ronald was tripping out after he said that. (pp. 345 TT)

Elizabeth was beside herself with fear. To quote her, "I was pissing and crying and pissing and crying. Pee Wee was acting crazy, you know."

Gregory, annoyed with the whole situation and Ronald's craziness, pretended to be drunk and walked away from both of them. Elizabeth didn't want Gregory to leave but wouldn't leave with him or didn't feel she could leave Ronald the way he was acting. (pp. 343, 684 TT)

Elizabeth got back in the car with Ronald, and they drove after Gregory. When they saw a group of people at Union and Hodiamont, in St. Louis, Elizabeth tricked Pee Wee and told him, "Hey there's Jay! (Gregory's nick name.)" She really hadn't seen Gregory; she only wanted Ronald to stop so she could get away from his craziness. During the time that Elizabeth and Ronald were alone, Ronald reached under the car seat and pulled-out ammunition, and reloaded the gun. (This information is in a taped interview with Elizabeth and never came out in the trial.) Elizabeth jumped out of the car and ran into the crowd. After Elizabeth left, Gregory, who really was in the crowd, got in the front seat of the car and the boys drove off. Elizabeth tried to warn Gregory before he got in the car that Ronald was acting crazy again, but she never told him that Ronald had reloaded the gun. (pp. 354, 685 TT; video tape interview of Elizabeth) Ronald had driven a short distance when Gregory asked, "Where are you going?"

"I'm going to Diane's house," Ronald said.

Gregory wanted to go home, but because he wasn't driving, he went along with Ron. It was while they were en route to Diane's that the decision was made to pick up Diane and a cousin, which would cause the car to be full. In the back seat, where Gregory had been sitting earlier, was a basketball and a partially full gas can with a hole in it. Ronald had brought the gas for Gregory's car, which was sitting empty at his house with a fuel line leak. All this time the gun was not visible. Gregory thought Ronald had put it in the trunk.

Once at Diane's apartment (a condemned building with several empty apartments), Gregory decided to take the gas can up to Diane's to store it out of the way in the empty apartment across the hall from Diane's so the fumes would not fill the car. He didn't suggest putting it in the trunk, because he thought the gun was there and didn't want to draw Ronald's attention to it, besides there was a hole in the gas can.

Once upstairs the brothers knocked on Diane's door. Diane was in her nightgown when she opened the door. She had been sleeping on the couch. Two men were with her in her apartment that neither Gregory nor Ronald knew. Five children were sleeping in the only bedroom. Andrew Chambers, one of the two visitors, had been the one who woke Diane up. She asked him to answer it, but according to Diane's testimony neither man could move, but also according to her testimony, they hadn't been drinking nor using drugs either. The two men in Diane's apartment were Bruce Campbell (the murder victim) and Andrew Chambers, a wounded bystander. When Gregory and Ronald entered the apartment, the smell of drugs lingered in the room. Diane and her sister had been drinking and smoking marijuana [laced with PCP] earlier that evening. (pp. Pages 291-292, 470, TT and Andrew Chambers" deposition [CD] which was not at the trial.)

The Oliver Brothers entered the apartment where the odor of burning PCP lingered. Gregory, knowing the reputation of the neighborhood and Diane, saw two men he didn't know and began copping an attitude as he often did around Diane, "I'm Jake the #^*%%#@#^* snake and there ain't no one bad as me." Then he asked if she was ready to go. Diane got off the couch and went to the bathroom to get dressed as if she were going to go with the boys. During that time, Bruce Campbell offered Gregory a drink out of the bottle he had in his brown paper bag. (TT, CD)

When Diane came out of the bathroom Ronald went in to use it. While Ronald was in the bathroom, Gregory and Diane went into the hallway to talk for approximately fifteen minutes. (pp. 470, 498, 502, 698-90 TT)

Diane testified that Gregory splashed gasoline all over the floor threatening to burn the place up while asking for a match to set it on fire when he entered the apartment. She also testified that she had wrestled the gas can away from him (Diane was about 5'4" and Gregory is 6'3") Gregory declares that he never did or said those things and that there was no wrestling match with Diane. (pp. 471-72, TT)

13

In the Andrew Chambers' deposition, Gregory was throwing lighted matches at the gas can, indicating that "no" gas had been splashed on the floor or the fumes would have exploded. Interestingly Gregory, Andrew Chambers, and the bomb and arson squad's report, or lack thereof, all supported Gregory's testimony that there was no gasoline splashed on the floor, but the evidence and the testimony to support this never made it to the courtroom. The jury was only given Diane's testimony and the gas can was lost in the police property room, which constituted a broken chain of custody. Also, one of the policemen who testified was led into testifying that he smelled gasoline when there was neither gas nor the can in the apartment.

When looking at three of the four stories, they are supporting Gregory's version. The three differing stories indicate that witness credibility which became a real issue in this case. The prosecution brought forward too many versions of the gasoline story for the jury to wade through when trying to create a motive...that was not there.

After Gregory and Diane's conversation in the hall, they came back into the apartment. Diane still hadn't made her mind up as to whether she was going with Gregory and Ronald to go get money. Gregory frustrated told her, "You ain't going, I'm fixing to go, I got to go." He told Ronald as he walked out of the apartment, "Come on!" (pp. 694 TT) Ronald had exited the bathroom and was standing behind Bruce Campbell (the transcripts indicate that Ronald and Bruce Campbell were having angry words).

Gregory made it as far as the landing when he heard the first shot. He turned around, ran back into the apartment, and saw Bruce Campbell lying slumped backward over a stool. He was trying to figure out how Ronald got a loaded gun back in his possession because he thought it was in the car trunk empty.

Diane, who had been in the kitchen when the first shot was fired, began yelling at Ronald. Ronald swore he saw a shotgun [a loaded shotgun was found in the kitchen of the vacant apartment across the hall with a fresh blood swipe on the wall next to it.] in her hand and then Ronald shot Diane four times. All this time, Gregory was hysterically jumping up and down on the floor, telling Ronald, "You can't kill nobody, what is you doing!" (pp. 689, 698, 702 TT)

Andrew Chambers was the third victim of Ronald's shooting spree. He testified in the deposition that Gregory asked his brother, Ron, "What did he do that for," when Ronald shot the victims. [This is referred to as "excited utterance" and supports Gregory's testimony of mild hysteria on his part.]

The next thing Gregory knew, "Ronald ran out the door" and he ran after him asking him, "Why did you shoot those people." Ronald didn't answer he just got into the car and Gregory followed. During this time Gregory began to collect himself as they drove around and finally wound up at their aunt's house. (pp. 700 TT)

Ronald's Mental Condition

In the fall of 1983, Ronald Oliver was a young husband and father of one son. He was an architectural student at Kansas State University, in Manhattan, Kansas. During one of his semesters there, the hospital discovered that he had a lobe lesion on the right side of his brain. Surgery was performed at the then St. Mary's Hospital in Manhattan, Kansas. After surgery, he was sent back to St. Louis for a convalescent leave for six weeks so proper healing could take place. This healing process required a stress-free environment. About three weeks into his convalescent leave, Ronald was caught in a house fire where his wife and best friend were killed. He was found lying over his son's body, suffering from smoke inhalation. His son, Ronald Jr., survived.

From that time on, Ronald's mental capacity was never the same and neither was his temperament. He flew off into violent rages for no apparent reason even with family members. Four family members testified at the trial that he tried to hurt them for the smallest reasons. The state psychiatrists also testified to Ronald's *uncontrollable* behavior, hallucinations, and the hearing of voices.

In summation, Ronald went from being a college-going student to someone with an IQ of 65-70 who would trip out and go off into violent outbursts. His change was drastic, so much so that the jail and prison authorities had to keep Ronald on the drug Mellaril, an antipsychotic drug, to control his temper.

Contradictions and Evidence

During the controversial parts of the testimonies, siding with Gregory's version of the story was much easier, because of the stability of his testimony and the lack of validity of Diane's testimony. During several out-of-jury-range discussions held by the prosecution, defense, and court during the course of the trial, the prosecution insulted and ridiculed Diane numerous times, saying he questioned her intelligence; yet he insisted that her character not be an issue in the trial and that the smoking of drugs not to be brought up. Also in transcripts, prior to the beginning of the trial, the prosecutor stated that he saw nothing in the record indicating that Gregory was guilty of any criminal action except that he had a gas can that he already admitted to.

16

Diane [the only eyewitness to testify] was shown by the state itself to be incompetent as a witness. Gregory was shown [by the same state attorney] to have an unimpeachable testimony that is why he brought in a rebuttal witness to try and impeach Gregory. When actually his testimony supported Gregory's testimony. Yet, the court and the jury took Diane's word over Gregory's even though nowhere in the transcripts did Gregory's ability to testify ever enter the conversation in a negative light. In the out-of-jury-range discussion, prior to the prosecutor calling the last rebuttal witness, the fact that Gregory's testimony had not been impeachable after 28 witnesses was a critical issue to the prosecution and is why he felt he needed to impeach Gregory.

The Trial

The Oliver brother's trial began with the pre-trial conference on April 6, 1987, which was twenty-two months after their arrest on June 6, 1985. This was a violation of the Federal "Speedy Trial Act". The cases against Ronald and Gregory were joined together, thereby making it impossible for Gregory to be the focal point of his own trial. This hampered Gregory's right to a fair trial by joining his case with his brother's case and issues around the validity of his mental condition and his defense of mental disease and defect. The prosecution, during the summation, drew attention to Ronald's mental condition numerous times by making numerous comments to the jury to disregard Ronald's condition. Ronald was taking Mellaril [a psychoactive drug]. We found out later from the prosecutor that Ronald was given a double dose of Mellaril for trial. Ronald sat through the entire trial in a lethargic state with a blank stare on his face because of the drug.

Prior to the trial, Ronald spent six weeks at Fulton Diagnostic Center, which is the psychiatric center for violent mental cases, under ideal conditions where he was tested for mental disease and defect. They concluded that he indeed was suffering from Organic Brain Syndrome. All tests proved positive. (pp. 843-924 TT) Since incarceration, originally at Missouri State Penitentiary at Jefferson City, Missouri, Ronald spent over one year undergoing further tests at Fulton, under those same ideal conditions. These tests proved that a portion of his brain was indeed dead from the combination of the surgery and smoke inhalation.

The focus of the Oliver brother's trial was on trying to build a case of pre-meditation based on the inconsistent statement of Elizabeth [the alleged kidnap victim] to four hearsay on hearsay witnesses. The prosecution tried to manipulate the statute with the agreement of the judge to establish something that wasn't there. There was no pre-meditation because there was no knowledge of the two men. Ronald was being charged with the kidnapping of Elizabeth, but Gregory was not being charged with kidnapping even though Elizabeth told the court she wasn't kidnapped.

When the jury came back with a verdict, they found Gregory guilty of First-Degree Murder, First Degree Criminal Assault, and Kidnapping. But what's this—Gregory wasn't charged with kidnapping—how could they find him guilty of it. The judge should have called a mistrial right then and there because of the jury confusion, but instead, he just brushed it aside and proceeded with the sentencing.

Both men received the maximum penalty of life without parole for first-degree murder and life with parole for first-degree criminal assault. Ronald received an extra 15 years for kidnapping Elizabeth even after she told the judge and prosecution that she was not kidnapped and did not want to press charges against either one of the brothers. (pp. 328-29 TT)

The bomb and arson squad were at the investigation scene taking samples, yet they did not testify at the trial. Why? Because there was no gasoline spilled on the floor. If they had, they would have been able to give the information as to whether gasoline had been poured out on the floor. If it had been found, the state would have had them as a witness to back up Diane's false testimony. There were no supportive witnesses to this fact. It was Diane's word against Gregory Oliver's word through the entire trial...a typical he said, she said scenario.

Charges were dropped to the First-Degree Criminal Assault against Andrew Chambers. The reason for this is because he could not be located. There is more to that story, but it never revealed itself until many years later. That is when we discovered that Andrew Chambers was the DEA's highest-paid narcotics snitch., and he was working with the transporting of drugs between California and St. Louis. His drug of choice was PCP—that is why he was at Diane's house that night. It is also why; the DEA wanted the charges dropped for the second 1st-degree criminal assault. They had to keep his activities quiet. The DEA often protected him as noted in the redacted DEA file on him.

CHAPTER 3
Gregory's Family
by
Gregory

I was born in St. Louis, Missouri May 2, 1956. I was the oldest of my father's second family. My father's first wife died. I had three half-brothers Reginald, Charles, and Columbus Jr. Reginald died a violent death, and Columbus Jr. died early of liver complications. My father, Columbus, was a businessman and taught all of us to be in business for ourselves and not rely on others or the government. My father was 56 when he married my 19-year-old mother Leanna, who was the oldest of nine children and took a lot of abuse growing up taking the punishment for her siblings regardless of her guilt for her sibling's actions.

From the very beginning, my mother said that everyone mentioned my smile when I walked into a room. Even in prison I had that reputation of smiling a lot. Being the oldest, I was also blessed to have more of my father's influence in my life than my younger brothers. As the oldest, I always had the caretaker role towards my siblings, and I felt I had to take responsibility for my siblings. I was not only the oldest but the largest of my siblings. I had two nick names when I was growing up. They called me "Jay" for Jay Bird, because I talked all the time and "Baby Huey" because of my size and awkwardness. I went into the Army as an enlisted man and served two enlistments, a total of six years, receiving two "Honorable Discharges." I wanted to try my hand at being a businessman when I got out of the service.

After me came Stanford, he was educated in the Catholic school and a white teacher took a special interest in him because she saw a bright future in him. He went on to obtain an engineering degree and became an officer in the United States Army retiring as a Lt. Colonel. He then went on to build a successful business upon his retirement from the military. Stanford and I had a similar look but he was thinner than I. None of my brothers were large like me.

Then came Ronald, he was darker skinned than I. He was small framed but quite wiry. He used to box a lot as a youth and sparred with the Spink's brothers growing up. He was a man of few words. Ronald married the love of his life; Joyce and they had a son Lil' Ronald. He wanted to follow in Stanford's footsteps and started going to Kansas State University to acquire a degree in Architecture. His education was cut short because of a tragic house fire that took the life of his wife and best friend at a time when Ronald was recovering from brain surgery for a lobe lesion. He suffered smoke inhalation and from that day forward he went from being a college student to being borderline retarded with an IQ of about 65. He would fly off the handle and go into violent rages trying to kill anyone in his way [friend, family or foe]. To commit him to an institution, my mother, who was now the head of the household, would have to gain custody of a grown man, but she never did it. By this time, my father was over 80 and dying of cancer.

Then came Christopher who got in trouble when he was young and went to prison. Christopher looked like me but was a smaller version when he was younger, but as he got older his looks changed. After getting out of prison,

Christopher too, went into business for himself as an auto mechanic. He runs a busy shop today.

Michael was darker skinned like Ronald and smaller framed; then came, Deborah, the only sister and the pride of my father's eye. Mark was the youngest, he had a similar look to me but was another smaller version, and was born when my father, Columbus Oliver, was in his 70's.

Growing up we had lots of aunts, uncles, and cousins around. So, when we got together, we were almost too many to count. To this day we have annual family reunions from my mother's side. We didn't know a lot about my father's side of the family. One of my brothers has a picture of my father when he was young, and he was quite the handsome fella. My mother was small framed all her life and was very pretty.

Gregory...fond memories of his Parents

Before I tell you about my parents, it needs to be noted that because I was in a maximum-security prison when they passed away, I was not allowed to attend either of their funerals. When the pandemic hit the world, millions of people were not allowed to attend funerals of their loved ones. I remembered how saying "goodbye" to my parents was taken away from me and how much my heart went out to all those people who couldn't say "goodbye" either and I understand how they felt.

When my brother Ronald died at the prison and after all of the arrangements were made by my family, I was not allowed to attend his funeral either.

✝

As a parent, my daughter was one year old when I was arrested. For the twenty-two years and five days. Those formative years were taken from me. Her first steps, her first word, her first tooth and all the firsts that a child goes through. The sad thing of all this is it wasn't about justice. It was a power issue of people who would go to any length to concoct a story and still refuse to admit their wrong. It has always been said that the cover up is worse than the crime that someone does.

✞

My mother and father were decent people. My mother was from Tennessee my father was born shortly after the turn of the 20th century in Mississippi, so he witnessed many things my mother didn't. My father was a man of strong character and was a very devout family man. He was a businessman and Baptist preacher. He would be appalled at what is going on today. He used to own three lumber yards when he was younger and built a church in Illinois that is still standing today. He believed in the Word of God and prayer. He would caution me about some of the people that I would hang around with. He had an ability to see my friends' character before I did.

He took me everywhere and would let everybody know I was his son. He would pat me on the head and say with pride. "This is my son!" With these outings he taught me how to handle business ethics and how to interact with people of all walks of life. I learned the strength and need for prayer. My father would tell me when I was being mischievous, "Boy, you'd better get in here and pray." The Bible says to "*train up a child in the way he should go and when he becomes old he will not depart from it.*" My parents believed that with all their hearts.

My dad taught me to walk softly when you find yourself in a lion's den. Little did he know the lion's den that I would find myself in. He taught me how to stand up to the bullies. He taught me to build my own business and not to rely on others. One time I remember when he was teaching me to love work. It was the middle of winter, and the drive shaft was broken on the car. He had me get under the car in the cold and he told me "Hey boy, get up under there take those bolts loose and take that drive shaft off there."

"But it is cold out!"

"Go on boy, I'm teaching you how to be a man."

My mother before she got her GED cleaned house for a rich white family. Her employers treated her and all of us like family. They gave us full reign of the house. We sometimes ate there, but the most fun was when they let all of us come over and swim in their pool. We weren't taught racism we were taught what the family of God was. After she got her GED, she began working at the Post Office and that job provided for our family when my father was too old to work.

My mother was a good cook and we had good food. My father eventually had a job down at Soulard Market and he would make sure we had plenty of good food.

With everything my parents imparted in me the best thing was to trust in the Lord and to study the Word was the most valuable. They made me prepared for what I was to go through. We must live a prepared life.

CHAPTER 4
St. Louis City Jail
by
Gregory

The stench of urine, feces, and sweat from incarcerated men filled the air as a jailor led my brother and I to the cells we would be in until they processed us into the system. Once the iron door banged shut behind us, the only thing we had to look forward to was a cold bologna sandwich, watered-down Kool-aide, or coffee until after we were processed.

Once processed, we were able to move around more freely. We would have periods of recreation and library time in a small cell-like space that was full of legal books. We could attend church services and there were classes available that were sponsored by the St. Louis Public Schools for those inmates who needed to get their GED.

Little did I know that this would be my home for the next 22 months while I awaited trial. Jail time is the time where a perspective felon earns his reputation that carries on to the penitentiary. In some ways, it is harder than prison because the men have not even been convicted yet. If an inmate can't stand in jail, then he will be considered weak, and that weakness will precede him when he walks into prison. You could just be walking along and be attacked for no reason.

This was a way of testing the new inmate to see if you could or would stand strong. Even the administration segregated the jail based on the maturity of the strength of the inmate. If you could prove that you could handle yourself, you were placed in the toughest level of the jailhouse where the more aggressive inmates were housed. If an inmate could not handle himself aggressively, then he was put in an area with the less aggressive inmates or in protective custody...depending upon their needs. In those cases, the only time they had any contact with an aggressive inmate would be in church service or classes, which were held apart from protective custody.

There was a mental ward in the jail that shared part of the sixth floor. These inmates required daily medication to keep them under control. This is where my brother Ronald was housed because he was taking Mellaril, an antipsychotic drug that aided in controlling his temper. On this drug, Ronald was very lethargic and somewhat unresponsive.

I was housed on the fifth floor with the older and more aggressive inmates after I had proven myself. Each day was a challenge once the doors to our cells were open. One day there was an incident because a group of men wanted to escape. They had a visitor smuggle in some hack saw blades through a hole that was up under the visiting room window on the fifth floor. This made it easy for the inmate to remove the blades when he was in the visiting area. This hole was also used for passing drugs to the inmates. For weeks, the men continued to saw a hole in the wall of the bedroom area which leads to the back hall, where they would cut the bars to make good their escape through the window. To do this the inmates worked while the guards were on duty during the day. They would turn the radio up full blast to hide the sound of the sawing. This went on for weeks until one day one of the inmates asked me if I was going with them. I told him, "No!"

He became outraged and said, "If you ain't going, then you gonna snitch on us."

I told them, "I don't care what you all do...I'm not going!"

But he wouldn't let this go and so he came at me with some sort of blade. To keep him from stabbing me I threw a mattress in his face and disarmed him. Because of the disruption, we both wound up in the hole.

We finished our time in the hole and went back to the fifth floor where the inmates were still working on their plan to escape. Their plan was interrupted because their blaring radio led the correctional officers to search the cell blocks. They found the used hack saw blades, which by that time were so worn down you couldn't tell what they were. They took all of us to the hole for having contraband of an unknown sort. After our time in the hole, they split us up placing us into different housing units. Years later I discovered if you ever have an escape attempt on your record it will kill any chance of appeal. I knew that being an innocent man...I had no reason to escape, I was to wait on the promises of God to deliver me.

I spent a great deal of time going to the library to study my case. I was searching for case law that would help my situation. In my pursuit, of the right law, I discovered that the law was only good for cases where the inmate was already convicted and had to have his case reversed. I needed to find a law that would help an innocent man before conviction. As I studied, it became clear to me that most cases like mine would not have even reached this point. I learned that mere presence or the flight thereof does not make one guilty of a crime. I studied hundreds of cases pertaining to this and accomplice liability, and each time I would try and place myself in the place of one of these cases where the person was guilty and I couldn't, because the law did not apply to my case.

I questioned *what accomplice liability was*? Under the Law, one is liable if he or she acts in concert with another in the commission of a crime. There must be active participation in the commission of that crime. It needs to be clear and concise evidence that the acting parties wanted a crime to come about. The act of mere presence, nor the flight thereof, does not make one liable of acting in concert. Unfortunately, too many people think that if you are present when a crime happens that you must be an accomplice to a crime. Nothing could be further from the truth. This lack of knowledge has kept many innocent people from *"Walking Free"*, *"Ignorance of the law is no excuse."*

My first step to *"Walking Free"* was to understand what I was being accused of, and this was difficult because in every innocent person's case the State seems to have a problem with the motive. This principle plays out in many cases where an innocent person is being charged. When Jesus went before Pontius Pilate, even Pilate questioned the accusations brought against the Lord, by saying *"I see no fault in this man."* But, because it was clear that the Lord was to be crucified for our sins, he did not defend himself. In my case, there were so many difficulties with establishing motive that the State's Attorney had to amend the indictment multiple times to try and fit the accusations to the crime. Therefore, the law guarantees that a defendant has the right to confront his accusers. In my case, I was not allowed to confront any of my accusers, first, because the trial was rigged as the Lord had shown me, and second, the accusations were always shifting. When the Lord assured me that this case against me was 'rigged', I was angered. Once I had received that revelation from the Lord, He did not stop there he began to educate me on how the court manufactured evidence and framed me for a crime I did not commit. Then he began to give me and my advocate the tools to pursue the right course of action for me to be "*Walking Free*" first, and then to clear my name.

The Lord showed me that He moves in steps and stages. The reason He does is because when he is done, we would have developed a lasting character from the experience. If he had performed a quick miracle, what benefit would it be to building character? The Lord's concern is our growth, maturity, and the knowledge and the gain through the test and trials we experience so that we would understand how the Lord comforts us so we may comfort others.

CHAPTER 5
The Good Samaritan
by
Gregory & Bonnie

*A*nd Jesus answering said, A certain [man] went down from Jerusalem to Jericho, had fallen among thieves, which stripped him of his raiment, and wounded [him], and departed, leaving [him] half dead. And by chance there came down a certain priest that way: and when he saw him, he passed by on the other side. And likewise, a Levite, when he was at the place, came and looked [on him], and passed by on the other side. But a certain Samaritan, as he journeyed, came where he was: and when he saw him, he had compassion [on him], And went to [him], and bound up his wounds, pouring in oil and wine, and set him on his own beast, and brought him to an inn, and took care of him. And on the morrow when he departed, he took out two pence, and gave [them] to the host, and said unto him, Take care of him; and whatsoever thou spendest more, when I come again, I will repay thee. Which now of these three, thinkest thou, was neighbour unto him that fell among the thieves: And *he said, He that showed mercy on him. Then said Jesus unto him, Be, and do thou likewise.* (Luke 10:33-37 KJV)

I sat in the city jail in St. Louis praying that God would send someone to believe in my innocence. It would take someone who could cut to the quick and see the real me. While at the city jail, Ronald and I only got to see each other at the church services or during the classes held for the GED and Adult Continuing Education program held there at the jail. The reason for the little bit of contact was because Ronald was housed on the 6th floor which was the psychiatric wing while I was housed on the fifth floor, which housed the older more seasoned inmates.

My favorite program at City Jail was the GED program. Both Ronald and I had our high school education, so they waved rules so that we could go to the class, and I could see Ronald and make sure he was alright. The program had a paid director and several volunteers that would come in on alternating days to help. I wanted to keep up with math. So, I asked the instructor if I could keep my mind sharp and work on math. Because I already had my GED, he offered me an assistant instructor's position so I could help the other men until a guard complained and I had to stop my tutoring, but I was kept in the class working on math and I was able to see my brother.

Other volunteers came in on a regular basis. This one day a woman came in she was well dressed as a businesswoman. She was working as a tutor, and I found out that her strongest skills were in math. I thought she could help me sharpen my skills.

We had been locked up at city jail for twenty months already when this woman started with the GED program. She did not seem to fit in. I first noticed her when she was on the elevator when it stopped at each floor handing the floor guard the list of men who could go up to the classroom. After a couple of weeks of her tutoring, she came up to me and told me, "You're special...you don't belong here." I looked at her and she looked at me. That was very refreshing because I had been praying "Lord I know there is someone out there who would believe in my innocence." Her name was Ms. Bonnie. She really encouraged me and let me know that God had answered my prayers. She even came to my trial. She slipped into the back. When I saw her, I nodded at her in the back of the room. What was interesting was that Ms. Bonnie was an ordinary person that cared enough for someone that was unjustly convicted. I did not even know how much she knew about my case. I was so really touched by this interaction. I was so excited that I had to share the experience with my mother. "Hey mom, this woman came up to me last night and told me I didn't belong."

Ms. Bonnie was kind to the men even though she was in an environment that was strange to her seeing all the men were mostly black. She looked at first like she was mean with a natural scowl on her face, but then when she smiled the fear of her scowl subsided for all of us. I think she was feeling uncomfortable in the environment she was in.

People today talk about systemic racism, but they are not correct. There are people in places who are racist but not everyone. Just like the Bible says a little leaven, leavens the whole lump. In today's world the expression is "one bad apple ruins the whole bunch." When one person introduces negative behavior others can choose through courage to halt it or through cowardness to allow it. We have to confront the errors of injustice; we have to overcome evil with good. Although Ms. Bonnie was a bit uneasy at first, she displayed no racial biases even when the men ran her through the wringer to see what she was made of. She proved herself of strong character.

Ms. Bonnie, by having the character of the "good Samaritan" was willing to overcome evil by confronting injustice with courage and the good within herself.

> *"Courage is an inner resolution to go forward despite obstacles; Cowardice is submissive surrender to circumstances. Courage breeds creativity: Cowardice repressed fear and is mastered by it. Cowardice asks the question, is it safe? Expediency asks the question, is it politic? Vanity asks the question is it popular? But conscience ask the question, is it right? And there comes a time when we must take a position that is neither safe, nor politic, nor popular, but one must take it because it is right."* Dr. Martin Luther King Jr.

Ms. Bonnie coming to the jail reminded me of an incident that happened to me many years ago when a stranger walked up to me on my street. He said to me, "You are going to go through many things, but you are going to come out, you are going to be a wealthy man, but they are going to be trying to take it from you, yet they are not going to be able to do it.

I said, "You have to be talking about somebody else."

He insisted, "I'm talking about you. Don't you stay in that house up there?" And he pointed to my mother's house.

I stated, "How do you know me?" Then he walked away without answering.

by
Bonnie

My first day at City Jail was indeed an experience. As we ascended to the sixth floor in an old iron bar elevator where classes were held; sometimes we could view two floors at a time. The elevator operator stopped at each floor and handed a list of inmates' names through the iron bars to the guard on duty. On the sixth floor, you stepped out into a large empty room. In the center of the floor was a trap door, and high above it was the rigging that had been used during the days when hangings were performed in the jail. It is said that the sound of the trap doors swinging open used to echo throughout the whole building, and a gruesome spirit of death would fill the cell areas, affecting all occupants.

Just to the left of the elevator as we stepped off was the multipurpose room, where classes were held. At one end of the room was a gym set with weights for the men to exercise on. A glassed-in guard station was on the center of the wall opposite the elevator, with doors on either side of it that led to the psychiatric wing. Bookshelves with our supplies on them, surrounded by bars, were back in a corner behind the gym set. There were four eight-foot tables where the men sat. Each table seated six men. There were always a couple of minutes prior to the start of class for the men to enter the room one floor at a time. The jail population maxed out at 625 men.

The statistics of the men at City Jail were ninety to ninety-five percent of the jail's population was black males and eighty to eighty-five percent of the crimes in question were murder and/or rape.

The more I came to the jail the more I learned about the street and its people. I thought it strange that I kept walking in on conversations about the Oliver brothers. It seemed that one was mentally impaired and the other was innocent. What bothered me was that no one seemed to want to help or fight for the innocent man even though he was liked by everybody in authority except one sneaky guard, Sam who no one liked.

There were several men I wanted to help but the more I got to know them the more I realized that they were indeed guilty of their crimes. Only one of the original inmates did I believe to be truly innocent and only one to be mentally impaired and that was Gregory and Ronald Oliver.

It was nearing time for the trial, and Gregory's mother had finally gotten Gregory a paid lawyer three months before the trial. Prior to that, he had three different Public Defender's during the nearly two years he was kept at St. Louis City Jail. Only one of the Public Defenders had met with Gregory for an hour during his jail time. Gregory's case came up for trial shortly after his arrest, but the Public Defender who was assigned to Gregory's case never showed up at the trial and it was after this mishap that the brother's cases were joined together. Ronald had a paid lawyer from the beginning. Gregory had to rely on public defenders. Gregory's mother finally got him a paid lawyer three months before trial. Gregory's lawyer was half the price of Ronald's lawyer, and it was his first capitol felony case.

One night just before Gregory's trial started, I was talking to one of the other volunteers and he was telling me about going to one of the inmate's trials.

"You mean we can go and watch the trial?"

"Sure, it is open to the public," He said.

My mind started working overtime. It was common knowledge to nearly everyone at the jail that Gregory was innocent, consequently, I was curious about his trial. I felt this uncontrollable urge to say something to Gregory other than talking to him about algebra. He indicated he needed help and I went over to his table and knelt down. I had my head down looking at his math book and was upset. There was this unquenchable urge to say something to Greg, but I did not know what. All I knew was that I was fighting back uncontrollable tears that seemed to be coming from deep down inside me. I did not know what was happening to me. Finally, I whispered to Gregory, "I have to say something after I help you, but I can't now." Then I went on to help him with his math problem. I didn't know what I was going to say or how I was going to say it. I just knew I had to say something. I finished helping him and immediately stood up looking right down into his eyes. "Young man," I said in a motherly tone. "You are special, you don't belong here. I want you to know I am praying for you." Tears flooded his eyes and were sucked back just as fast so none of the other inmates could see the telltale tears that would have run down his cheek. I could not believe I made this man cry. I never prayed. At that point I didn't know what to do so I just patted him on the shoulder and walked over to the other inmates to see if anyone needed help. I could feel Gregory's eyes on me all the way over to the other table.

It was April 15, 1987. I had a business appointment downtown with one of the other salespeople from my regular job. I planned to stay downtown to go to the Oliver brothers' trial, so I made an excuse to take my own car. My anxiety level was high, but I tried to rationalize it away by telling myself, "I am just a public spectator, nothing else."

I arrived at the courthouse about 11:30 A.M. Not wanting to be seen, I took a sneak peek through the glass doors. The courtroom was empty! I turned to walk away, and I ran into the bailiff "Can I help you?" he asked.

"I'm looking for the Oliver trial."

"This is it. They broke for lunch just a little while ago and will reconvene at 1:00 P.M. They'll begin the summation then."

"This might sound silly—I teach the boys over at the jail, and I have taken an interest in their case. I really don't know why."

"Oh, that happens a lot."

"How is it going?"

"I believe the big guy is going to walk, or at least get a lighter sentence. He got on the stand and testified the other day and did a good job."

"The big guy is the one I'm concerned about. Rumor has it he is innocent and didn't murder anybody."

"No, he didn't. I—uh—I really can't say which way it will go; you never know what a jury will do. As soon as you think you have one of these cases figured out, the jury rules differently. It could go anyway."

"Is it okay if I sit in on the summation?"

"Sure. It's an open courtroom."

"I really don't want Gregory to see me if you know what I mean. Is there somewhere I can sit and not be noticed?"

"Well, let's see. The way he is sitting at the table he could hardly keep from seeing you because his head turns every time the door opens. But you know, if you sit in the back to the far left while facing the bench, you'll be less noticeable."

"Thank you. Are the boys here now?"

"Yes. They're in a holding room, so they have no idea you're here."

"So, I can come back, and no one will give me any trouble for observing."

"Not at all. They begin at 1:00 sharp."

"Thank you, sir."

I left and went to lunch. I couldn't believe the timing. I got there just in time for the summation and closing arguments, so I would get the details of the case without having to sit through the whole trial. What a break! I had mixed emotions. I was thrilled because I was about to witness a murder trial in person; yet, because of the situation, I was fearful, seeing I personally knew the defendants.

I arrived shortly before 1:00 o'clock. There was a woman sitting where I wanted to sit, so I tried to get as inconspicuous as I could.

This courtroom was long and narrow. Because of its location, there was only one aisle, directly in line with the door. There were half a dozen wooden bench seats on either side of the aisle, separate from the trial area, for the spectators. Defense and Prosecution were at the same large table, which was positioned, so it followed the elongated floor plan of the room. The bailiff's station was to the left and the juror's section to the right. The judge's bench was set at an angle to get a fuller view of the room.

I didn't look as the door behind me opened—it was the boys. I was sure they didn't see me as they entered, and I slouched deeper in my seat, hoping to go unnoticed as they sat down. I saw Gregory's profile. He turned his head to nod to his family. I was several rows behind his family. As his eyes met his mother's, he caught glimpse of me. He twitched in surprise, trying not to react, and then he grinned and nodded. When he sat down, he leaned over to Ron. From my angle, I could read his lips as he said, "Bonnie's here." Then he turned and looked at me again.

The summation began. It was exceptionally long because they were trying two men together and both defense lawyers had their turn and the prosecution received two turns—one for each defendant. I listened intently, trying not to miss a beat. Ronald's lawyer was the most impressive of the bunch, but none of the lawyers impressed me that much—I was expecting high courtroom drama (too much TV, I guess). Something about the judge bothered me. I could not put my finger on it though. Regularly, Gregory would turn and look at me. I think he was looking for my reaction.

By the time the closing arguments were complete, there was no doubt in my mind that Gregory did not murder anyone. It was about 4:30 P.M. when they finished and released the jury to deliberate. Once the jury left the room, the boys were ushered out, and they had to walk right past me. Gregory's eyes were fixed on me. I saw a woman a couple of rows ahead of me reach out and grab his hand, and I followed suit. I reached my hand out to Gregory, and he grabbed it tight and didn't let go until he couldn't hold on any longer. My hand was over my head backwards; my arm stretched as far as it could go.

While the jury was deliberating, I went back to work, but I couldn't concentrate on anything. I made an excuse as to why I couldn't attend the special meeting that evening for our new insurance program and headed back to the courtroom to await the verdict.

Inside the courthouse, I went back to the courtroom to wait. The empty courtroom was eerie, and I was restless, so I walked across the hall. I saw a small black woman sitting alone. I asked her if she knew the boys, and she said, "I'm their mother."

I introduced myself and asked if I could sit with her. She said, "Yes." I began to tell her why I was there and had such an interest in her sons.

"I saw you earlier and wondered who you were," she said. I continued talking with her, telling her about making Gregory cry. She stopped me by exclaiming, "You're the woman!"

"What do you mean?" I asked.

"Jay (Gregory's nickname, I found out) called me Friday morning and said, 'Mama there is a woman at the jail that told me I didn't belong here.' He told me, 'It was so spiritual, Mama. When I looked into her eyes, I knew God had sent her.' I knew he was right. God sent you." I smiled, and she went on, "You felt it too?"

"Yes, but I didn't know what it was."

"He didn't tell me you were white."

"Does that matter?"

"No."

The hours passed, and I got to know all the Oliver's who were present. There was a spell when I felt out of place with the family, so I moved into the courtroom just in time to hear the judge in casual conversation with the bailiff, court reporter, etc. He was telling them about the motion Gregory's lawyer had filed for a mistrial. I listened and watched carefully. Evidently, the request for a mistrial had 49 points [actually there were 50 points it was mis-numbered], stating why Gregory's lawyer thought it should be declared a mistrial. The judge was not pleased about it. "If he thinks this is going to change things," he said, "he's wrong. I'm going to deny his motion for mistrial."

I tried to view this judge as objectively as possible, there was an arrogance about him that repulsed me. Now I knew why he bothered me.

I was concerned with what I overheard. There had to be something wrong if a lawyer, even the worst lawyer, could come up with 50 different points to justify a request for a mistrial. One point is all it takes to call a mistrial. There had to be at least one of those points that had to be accurate.

Everyone in the room had seen me enter, so I couldn't be accused of eavesdropping. But outside of the bailiff, they had no idea who I was because I didn't show up until the last day. This was the beginning of a picture that was going to get bigger for me. I could not believe what I saw happening—to the Oliver boys, to the system, and to myself.

The verdict was in. There was a general scurrying about, trying to get everyone together who had an interest or part in the case to be present for the reading of the verdict. When the jury had been released for deliberation, the court had informed them that a guilty verdict would result in a life sentence without Probation or Parole on the murder charge in lieu of the death penalty, and a sentence of life with parole on the first-degree assault charge. In Ronald's case, there was an additional charge of kidnapping, and the court asked for an additional 12-15 years if a guilty verdict was returned on that charge.

Mrs. Oliver took a seat next to me in the courtroom. Anxiously, we all listened for the verdict. The jury only deliberated three and a half hours, and they were all taken out for dinner first, which is not normal procedure. I thought the deliberation time was ridiculously short, seeing the jury had about 26 issues to go over while making their decision.

The judge began reading the verdicts, charge by charge. I sat there dumbfounded; I simply could not believe the jurors' decisions. Guilty on this, guilty on that, and on and on the verdicts went. Whenever guilty verdicts are returned, the standard procedure is to rush the defendants from the room, not knowing how they will react. There is supposed to be no physical contact with anyone.

As they escorted the boys down the aisle, Gregory's eyes were riveted on me. I reached my hand out to him, and he reached for mine. The bailiff immediately leaned forward to stop the contact. As he did, his eyes met mine and he slowly backed off to let Gregory's hand grab mine just as he had before, hanging on for as long as he could. Something had stopped that bailiff from interfering with our contact. I knew it, but I could not explain it.

Mrs. Oliver just kept saying, "I'm not going to cry." Well, if she wasn't, I was—and I did.

In the background, I heard one of the lawyers telling the boys in the holding room, "I did all I could do." Who were they trying to kid? Gregory was innocent of murder, and Ronald had a provable mental condition—a condition so bad the prosecutor had to keep reminding the jury to disregard Ronald's blank stare in the courtroom because of the medication the state had him on—stuff they give to people who are psychotic. Justice? What justice? I cried most of the way home.

✝

Thursday came and instead of holding class, Vaughn, Pete, Steve (another volunteer), and I went out for pizza. I was livid as I told them about my experience the day before at the courthouse.

"Calm down, Bonnie," Vaughn said.

"What do you mean, calm down? That man is innocent!"

"We know it."

"How can you sit there and say, 'We know it,' and not be affected by it?"

"It happens all the time."

"That doesn't make it right," I protested.

"He'll filter through the system and eventually get out."

"What do you mean 'filter through the system?'" I asked.

"We see these guys come and go all the time," added Pete, as he joined in the conversation. "They eventually get out. Probably seven or eight years he'll get out."

"I can't believe what I'm seeing," I said. "Our system is so fouled up, and that judge—I couldn't believe what I heard him say—and that jury! How in the world could they sit there, hearing the same things I heard, and send that man away for the rest of his life—with no parole? It's not fair."

"We know, Bonnie," Vaughn said.

"Well, how can you sit back, and just say and do nothing?"

"There's nothing you can do."

"There has to be something—it's so unfair."

I was so frustrated when I went home. How can people know the truth and allow the lies to ruin a person's life? I knew I had to do something, but I did not know what. I fell asleep pondering it.

"You may never know what results come of your actions, but if you do nothing, there will be no results." Mahatma Gandhi

CHAPTER 6
My Trial & Appeal
by
Gregory & Bonnie

The trial finally began and the $5,000 lawyer that my mother eventually hired for me He told me, "Don't worry, you will be home by Friday." Many Fridays passed me by in the 22 years and 5 days I spent waiting for the Lord to fulfill his promise that I would be 'walking free' out of prison.

The trial was "rigged" from start to finish and there was so much going on that it took years to uncover the things hidden in the darkness around this case. It was like a "Gordian Knot[1]" so twisted that we did not know where to begin our own investigation?

The *first* glaring error and major problem were that the judge allowed the prosecutor to join my case with an Illegal joinder with my mentally ill brother's case. Because of this tactic, the Jurors were not able to compartmentalize the

---

[1] **Gordian knot, knot** that gave its name to a proverbial term for a problem solvable only by bold action. In 333 bc, Alexander the Great, on his march through Anatolia, reached Gordium, the capital of Phrygia. ... The phrase "cutting the **Gordian knot**" has thus come to denote a bold solution to a complicated problem.

evidence which made the case confusing with the way the prosecutor presented his concocted story. All the evidence was against Ronald and everything presented ran over onto me, consequently, I was not the object of my own trial. This was an illegal tactic that is called the "melt-down-affect". Our cases got joined about six months after the arrest. My first trial came up at the proper time. The prosecutor had already tried a few times to have the cases joined, but the judge refused to join our cases more than once. On the day of my trial, the public defender didn't show up. So that gave the prosecutor the opportunity to make a deal with the public defender to join the cases. The original charges for both my brother and I were charged with, 1 count of 1st degree murder, 2 counts of 1st degree of criminal assault, and 1 count of kidnapping. The prosecutor said he would drop the kidnapping charge against me if the defense would agree to join the cases. So, the deal was made unbeknown to me and that is how our cases got joined. Ten minutes before our trial began, the prosecutor nolle prose 1 count of 1st degree criminal assault against Andrew Chambers, which left the charges to 1 count 1st degree murder, 1 count of 1st criminal assault, and Ronald was charged with kidnapping.

The *second* glaring error and major problem were in the fact that the prosecutor tried the case on a statute of the inconsistent statement (491-074) against the alleged kidnap victim, Elizabeth. This statute, at the time of trial, was a *civil* statute that was used primarily when there were children involved and it allowed for hearsay testimony to be admitted. The use of this statute in 1986 was illegal to use in a criminal case. The transcripts revealed a discussion between the court, prosecutor, and defense counsel which indicated that the defense was arguing about the use of the statute. The judge who sided with the prosecution stated, "*if the defense is correct about the use of this, **then we are in trouble**.*" The use of this statute barred any chance for the defense to cross-examine Elizabeth properly. She was the woman they used as a scapegoat to fabricate lies against her and us by using hearsay-on-hearsay testimony.

Our appeals were separated and in one of the appeals decisions, the appeal judge stated that he hated this statute (491-074) because it gave room for **overzealous prosecutors and police officers to fabricate evidence**. Which is exactly what happened in my case. Fortunately, both Appellate Courts found the use of the statute to be an error, but they called it *'harmless error'* and the slippery slope the judge knew they would be on if they were wrong on the application of 491.074 proved to be an error. But were they in trouble? No, because trouble was waved by the court calling it *'harmless error.'*

The *third* glaring error came when the prosecutor impeached his own witnesses, more than once. Despite the objection from the defense, their objections were overruled. The prosecution was notorious for impeaching witnesses, primarily his own witnesses. At the end of the trial, the prosecution brought in two rebuttal witnesses to try and impeach my testimony. The first one was not directed at me but the second one was. The rebuttal witness was a 15-year-old boy who Ronald had roughed up while I was still in Elizabeth's apartment. Prior to the questioning, there was a discussion at the bench. The Defense was objecting to the young man testifying. The prosecution stated that he needed to be able to impeach my testimony. At that point, there had been 27 witnesses and the prosecutor had not able to impeach my testimony. He was hoping that the young man would be able to. The judge overruled the defense's objection and allowed the rebuttal witness. Lo and behold it backfired on the prosecution. The young man supported my testimony, which blew the prosecution's theory. My testimony was never impeached.

To win the case, the prosecution had to concoct a story and discredit Elizabeth's testimony. This was **the *fourth* glaring error**. The prosecution brought forward four hearsay witnesses, one of whom was a hearsay-on-hearsay witness; two of whom were unendorsed, one was a police officer who took the place of the bomb and arson squad and his area of expertise was not in the area of the bomb and arson squad. His testimony in the critical issues was in the form of leading questions. The state when building a case should not have to ask leading questions to its own witnesses. The other was a friend of all the victims except for Andrew Chambers. The use of unendorsed witnesses is equated to suborn perjury seeing the friend of the victims was related to the murder victim and it never came out at trial but was obvious in the prosecutor's notes.

In most trials, there is physical evidence that is brought before the jury to help in proving the case against the defense. In mine and Ronald's case, there was no gun or any physical evidence. All the prosecution had was a couple crime scene photos, but not all of them. It would take 30 years before we received the crime scene photos, which told a completely different story than the prosecutor's concocted story. This was **the *fifth* glaring error**.

Then there was a gas can that Ronald brought for me because my car had a gas line leak, and it was out of gas. I needed just a little to get it moving. I didn't want to leave the can in the back seat of the car because we were expecting to have four people in the car. I figured I could leave the gas can in the adjacent empty apartment so we could go out and get Diane some money she had called me collect about this earlier that day. The prosecution tried to use this as an attempted arson case against me with no physical evidence.

All he had was a picture of a gas can. The lab tech testified that he turned the gas can over to the Bomb and Arson Squad and that they lost it, which is a *broken-chain-of-custody*, therefore the picture of the gas can should not have even been allowed as evidence. This was **the *sixth* glaring error**. This is the only thing the prosecution was using to build a case against me of attempted arson and was how he was trying to connect me to the case.

He then tried to use jealousy as a motive for me to participate with my brother. Months earlier I use to go over to Diane's house for sex and that was the extent of our relationship. Diane's house was a drug house, and it was common for a lot of druggies to hang around there. There was no jealousy on my part when I saw the strange men in her apartment.

When the verdict came down the jury found me guilty of count 1 of 1st degree murder, count 2 of 1st degree criminal assault, and count 3 of kidnapping. KIDNAPPING? I wasn't charged with kidnapping. The judge realizing the error, because the jury could not compartmentalize the evidence of the two defendants, so the judge wiped the verdict aside and continued with setting a date for the sentencing. This was **glaring error number *seven*.**

by
Bonnie

The *eighth* glaring error was in the PCR [Post Conviction Remedy also known as the 29-15]. This is where the defendant who was convicted challenges the ineffectiveness of the defense attorney. There were four parties present, and it was held in a deposition form with the judge presiding, an appointed state's attorney, Gregory's appointed appeal lawyer, and Gregory's trial attorney. The appeal attorney questioned Gregory's trial attorney about everything. One of the things that came out was that Gregory's attorney testified that he had seen documentation that there was no gasoline spilled or splashed gas in Diane's apartment, which supported Gregory's testimony and negated the concocted story that Gregory was planning on burning the apartment down. At trial, the defense did little to nothing to disprove the arson theory by presenting the documentation he mentioned in the PCR.

We were waiting for the decision on the PCR and no news. On one of my trips to visit Gregory, I kept getting this compulsion that I had to go to the courthouse and see if there had been a decision on the PCR so we would know. The lady at the desk was nice to work with. As soon as I mentioned brothers, she knew the case. She checked her file and there was no decision yet. She told me to check back again. A decision had to be made on the PCR before the case went to the appeal court.

It was a few months later when I was passing through downtown St. Louis, and I thought I would stop in again to see if a decision had been made on the PCR. The clerk remembered me and when she checked the records it was there. They denied the PCR. Without hesitation, at my request, the woman printed me off a copy of the PCR free. What was so aggravating was that the attorney did not inform Gregory of the decision—I had to.

by
Gregory
Once the PCR was complete, it was time for the appeal. I was to have my own appeal and Ronald was to have his own, which supported the fact that we should not have been tried together in the first place. My appeal was held on March 15, 1990, in St. Louis. Bonnie was planning on being at the appeal hearing so we would not miss anything. Then

49

she was going to come to visit me and tell me the outcome from a spectator's view. This day is when **the *ninth* and *tenth* glaring** errors occurred. At the Appeal Hearing, there were three judges, Bonnie had told me that she had prayed about all three judges and the third one was going to be the difficult one. The Prosecution just argued timing issues that had nothing to do with my guilt or innocence. My attorney got up and argued the two critical issues in my case which were:

1. Gregory Oliver did not murder anyone, and
2. The critical issue, in this case, was why the judge upheld the jury decision.

To Bonnie's surprise, the judge agreed by saying, "You're right Gregory Oliver didn't murder anyone, and the critical issue is why the judge upheld the jury decision." Bonnie felt certain we were in until after my lawyer's argument. Suddenly, that same judge angrily struck out against Bonnie, saying, "Who is Bonnie Lou Stuck?" [**The *eleventh* glaring error**] She was sitting in the back of the courtroom observing. Eight days before trial, Bonnie, in one of her studies found the federal 'speedy trial act' and saw just how bad the state of Missouri violated this law so in her letter she argued it rebutting the state's argument on a timing issue. Then he said to my attorney, "Is she an attorney?'

"No, your honor, she is a divinity student."

"Did you put her up to writing this letter?'

"No sir I didn't."

"Well doesn't she know she has no business writing the court?"

Bonnie was floored! She had written several letters to the court and in each case, she received a letter back from the court clerk stating acknowledgment of the letter and letting her know it was going into the record. This proved she had every right to write letters to the court. My lawyer was upset with the confrontation with the judge and was concerned that she errored when she gave Bonnie a copy of the state's argument before the appeal, so she would know what they were arguing.

After the appeal hearing, Bonnie came to visit me so she could update me. I was anxious about her visit. She told me that they ran another security check on her when she came into the prison. I was glad to hear that the judge agreed with my lawyers that I didn't murder anyone and that the critical reason in the case was why the judge, who brushed aside the kidnapping verdict, had upheld the jury decision.

We had a good visit and after about 4 hours one of the CO's [correctional officer] came up to us and told Bonnie they wanted to see her up at the desk. As soon as she left, the CO came over and picked up her things and told me the visit was over. I tried to ask questions, but the guard was not answering any of my questions. I went down to my cell all the time concerned about what was happening to Bonnie. I got a couple of inmates together and we all prayed for her because I knew something was wrong.

Every time I had a chance, I tried calling her home with no answer. I knew the next day something was wrong when she still wasn't answering her phone. Bonnie always drove straight through when leaving. I continued calling every hour with no success. Then finally at midnight, I tried again, and success Bonnie answered. "What happened?"

"I was arrested?"

"For What?"

"A dog off a leash from four years earlier when I lived in O'Fallon."

"You've got to be kidding!"

"No, I am not. I was handcuffed and driven back to O'Fallon over 100 miles to be rebooked and had another mug shot taken."

"They don't transport people over 25 miles unless they are known felons."

"They don't?"

"No, there is no reason for it."

"Oh, on top of it, there was no summons ever issued either. So, the officer issued her a summons dated the day after the warrant. Bonnie has proof that it was an erroneous warrant, and the warrant was issued on a four-year-old neighbor complaint." [**The *twelfth* glaring error**] I think they really wanted Bonnie to back off the case. I read the letter she wrote, and it was very pointed and challenging to the integrity of the lower court.

About ten years later Bonnie discovered that the judge that got angry at her letter writing was also the mentor of the trial judge and he never recused himself [**glaring error *thirteen* the number of judgments.**]

CHAPTER 7
Missouri State Penitentiary – MSP
by
Gregory

MSP earned the nickname "the bloodiest 47 acres West of the Mississippi River" and for years the name was well deserved for the behavior that went on behind those walls. I remember my first day behind the walls of MSP. We walked through the doors out into the population to get to our first assigned cells. Our first experience let us know what it was going to be like. They were rushing a man from the cell block to the infirmary. He was bloody from head to toe. To this day I still do not know if he survived the attack. Day in and day out this was a regular occurrence. It got so common that it did not matter where we were, the dining area, the recreation area, wherever. There was something in the air that let us know another incident was going to happen.

We were first assigned to three house. In three house there were four tiers of cells overlooking a wide-open space. There were no elevators, so to reach each tier you had to use the steps. If a fight broke out on one of the upper tiers, it was common to see a body falling over the rail sometimes to his death. It wasn't long before we realized that this place was no more than a gladiator school, where only the strong would survive. Some men made their own weapons from anything that they could get their hands on. Some weapons were more sophisticated because there were men who worked in the sheet metal shop who could make anything they wanted and slip it out into the population. A lot of the knives (shanks) would be buried in the yard area or hidden in various places throughout the prison hiding them from the guards. Some of them were eventually found but the men would just make more for whenever they felt they needed them. I never saw any guns or zip guns, but I knew they were on the premises, because the inmates would talk about them all the time. Some things were even brought in by guards who were bribed by the inmates.

Some of the houses were more dangerous than others and for Ronald and I, we stayed out of the other's way as much as possible because of the culture shock we were experiencing. I could see God's wisdom every step of the way getting us through this horrible ordeal, day by day.

After being at MSP for many years, it was a miracle I did not have any major incidents with other inmates that might have triggered violent behavior. As a matter of fact, it didn't dawn on me until now just how much the Lord had walked the halls before me. One day after 20 years in prison my cellmate said to me, "You must be soft...you haven't had a fight in 20 years!" That was not the case though. My survival was the favor of God, with the respect of inmates knowing not to bother me, and notwithstanding that my reputation had preceded me from the City Jail in St. Louis. I was known as the man that beat down Anthony Leisure, the mob boss, and it was he who gave me the nickname "Big O" which stuck throughout my prison time. The inmates know if you are known to fight someone of that stature that you are not to be messed with.

At night, you could hear the men screaming up on the upper tiers from men being raped, and sometimes all the guards would do, was to say, "Cut that noise out up there!" Young men hanging on the streets, in gangs, or participating in other bad activity do not know what they are in for when they are caught. In the prison setting especially if they are young. Some of them survive and some of them don't. If they don't know anyone, they have a hard time ahead of them. They don't have their oozies or AK-47's that they have been taught to use on the streets, so it is a whole new ballgame for them to have to adjust to. The old gangsters (OG) survived with their fists and knew how to handle themselves. They knew to never go into a fight when you are angry because you are apt to be blinded by your anger and that would cause defeat.

There is not much to do in prison except lift weights, run the yard, play the different sporting activities, go to the law library, attend church services, read, and at one time attend college programs until it was disbanded from the prison. They felt that a sentence of life without and life and 50 did not need an education. I spent a lot of time at church activities, using the law library, and I finished the Para Legal program earning my Associates Degree while I was in prison. I also played a lot of handball, which a well-known convict told me that I was going to earn a name for myself because I was a good player. We also played basketball to pass the time. Sometimes they would even allow college students to come in to play with us.

Seeing that this was a maximum-security prison, there were men that were incarcerated for anything from murder, kidnapping, pedophilia, rape, robbery, drugs, and a few serial killers. Missouri had a famous serial killer named Dr. Engleman who they made a movie about "*The Dentist*". He was also AKA "The Killing Dentist." He was exposed in a two-part documentary series *"The FBI Files."* He was very anti-social, and he refused to engage and talk with many inmates, but for some reason, he enjoyed talking with me. I think sometimes he would call himself mocking Jesus when I would tell him that he needed the Lord in his life. Some mornings after he got to know me more and more, he would love to see me and sometimes, jokingly would say, "I think I need to get Jesus in my life." One day I felt led to ask Dr. Engleman why he liked talking to me and he told me, "Because you got some sense." Being as intelligent as he was, I asked him, "Why did you kill all those people?" This was after I felt comfortable enough to ask him that question.

To my surprise, he answered, "Because I am a Hedonist and I live for pleasure." Normally we don't ask other people about their crimes or what led them into prison, but Dr. Engleman and I got the chance to talk quite often seeing he distanced himself from other people.

If you can look past the horrible things that he did, you could see him as your next-door neighbor. Maybe that is what allowed him to win his victim's trust over. He was your average everyday person; someone you could have coffee with, discussing the current events with, and you wouldn't think anything about it. In other words, with the educational background he had and his brilliance he was very likable. His case was so bad some of the other inmates were afraid of him.

There was another man named Jerry that I met at MSP that many of the inmates stayed clear of him. I didn't know his background, because I didn't ask him. He did tell me he was innocent. To make extra money, he would buy potato Chips, candy, and other food items and sell them to the inmates. Occasionally he would walk the yard a little, and he went to the library a lot to fight for his freedom. But for the most part, he was a loner. I would go to his cell and sometimes talk to him for hours. During this time, I was going to Jr. College through the prison system as a paralegal. One night I was running late for class. Like every inmate, God gave me an opportunity to minister to. Jerry, I ministered to him quite often and planted quite a few seeds as well as talking to him about the law. This night I wanted to stop and talk to him, but I had to get to class. When I saw him there was a real distance about him. I think the Lord was letting me know that was the last time I was going to see him. When I got back from class, the guards hollered up to the third tier and asked me, "Have you seen Jerry?" knowing that he didn't talk to too many other people. I told them "no, I just got back from class." Ten minutes after that the guards locked the whole prison down and 15-20 minutes later, they found Jerry dead in his cell. They hadn't seen him because he was found laying in his bunk and was covered up. They believed that he died of a heart attack because of the stress caused by the environment.

One of my highlights was my open visits that I was finally able to have with Bonnie and she would make the trip from O'Fallon, Missouri every other weekend. We would sit at the table, and we could pray. When I would come in Bonnie always had a pile of snacks waiting for me that she had bought from the vending machines. It was always a good visit because the only other contact we had was through letters and The telephone. We talked a lot about my case and strategies on how to approach it and which steps we needed to take. A lot of times we could see where the Lord had set the stage for the things we needed to address, and I know Bonnie spent hours in prayer seeking direction. There were times I wanted her to do something or speak to someone, but she would not budge until the Lord gave her the direction, which I thought was good. It meant she was hearing from the Lord. Every time she moved at His directive; things seemed to work out. I quickly learned if I was going to get her to do anything that I had to ask the Lord and let him tell her.

Missouri State Penitentiary—where I lived for about 15 years. I was housed on the third level.

For example, how and when we got married. We got married while I was still locked up. I didn't tell her that we needed to get married before her 50th birthday which was September 18th, or I was going to consider that she was not the woman who God wanted me to be with and move on with no hard feelings. Lo and behold Bonnie had me call her and told me to check as to when they were doing marriages at the prison. It just so happened that September was the only month they were allowing weddings to be done and the dates were September 7, 14, 21, 28. Now we had to be married before the 18th so there were only two dates that she could have selected to make this happen. She selected the 14th that is when I knew for sure that this was the woman the Lord wanted me to marry. We were married on September 14, 1994. Our God is truly the matchmaker.

The flower arrangement was done by my sister-in-law Barbara who was supportive of my fight to clear my name.

"Whoso findeth a wife findeth a good thing, and obtaineth favour of the LORD." (Proverbs 18:22)

CHAPTER 8
Ronald
by
Gregory & Bonnie

Gregory and Ronald celled together when Ronald was not being housed at the psychiatric hospital in Fulton, MO. During the day, those inmates that were on medication were given their meds to take by the dispensary. They would announce over the loudspeaker that it was time to take their medicine and the men would be supervised as they did. Many of the inmates were on antipsychotic drugs in order to keep them under control. Ronald was on Mellaril and had to take it a couple times a day to keep him under control. Ronald didn't like taking his drugs because he said, "it makes me too sleepy." For some reason, they gave Ronald his prescription drug relying on him to take his own medicine, which was unusual. They usually dispensed the medicine daily at medication time. Ronald sometimes was on his honor to take his meds, and on days where it was obvious when he had not. Gregory was indeed not only serving a prison sentence for a crime his mentally impaired brother committed but it felt like to him he was getting reprimanded when Ronald did not take his medication the way he was supposed to.

I am reminded of one visit when Gregory and I were talking about his case and innocence. I was shocked at something he told me;

"I knew I had to go to prison with Ron," Gregory said casually.

"What do you mean you knew you had to go to prison with Ron." I was curious about his comment.

"Well, you see, I was the oldest and I felt like it was my responsibility to look out for my younger brother."

"You are not responsible for anyone's actions but your own." I implored, "What made you think you had to go to prison for a mentally impaired brother?"

As our conversation continued, I began to realize that Gregory was raised to look out for his younger siblings, but going to prison with his brother and being his keeper? That was a bit much for me to comprehend.

Gregory and Ronald had a regular routine and would say their prayers together before they went to bed every night. This one night Gregory was troubled by Ronald's prayer and new he had not been taking his medication. Gregory knew Ronald was hallucinating while he was praying.

"I am not going to worship a machine." That is what Ronald said.

"A machine," Gregory thought, "what is wrong with him? I'll bet he forgot his medication."

Gregory soon fell off to sleep. About two A.M. he rolled over to see Ronald standing on his cot like a zombie. He called for the guards, who came running and they transported him to the prison hospital. After a couple of days in the hospital, Gregory was allowed to visit him. The first thing Gregory noticed about Ronald was his eye...it looked like it had been injured. Later Gregory found out that Ronald tried to scratch out his eye. He was following scripture in an abnormal way.

> "And if your eye causes you to stumble, gouge it out and throw it away. It is better for you to enter life with one eye than to have two eyes and be thrown into the fire of hell." (Matthew 18:9 KJV)

During most of the time that Ronald was in the hospital at the prison, they had him in a five-point restraining bed. After two weeks, they decided to transport Ronald to the Psychiatric Hospital. Two guards were escorting Ronald through the prison to put him in the van that was waiting to transport him to the hospital. Suddenly, Ronald started choking on a blood clot that he received from the restraining bed that broke loose. The guards didn't know what was happening and put Ronald into a chokehold. Ronald died before they even got him into the transport van. He was pronounced DOA when he arrived at the psychiatric hospital, not at the prison where eyewitnesses said he died after a wrestling match with the guards.

by
Gregory

To my understanding, if an inmate or a person dies any place due to suspicious circumstances the coroner must come on the scene to pronounce the time of death. This did not happen, which makes it look like the prison wanted to get the problem [Ronald] away from them now! He should have been transported two weeks earlier. During the time they kept him at the prison they were not able to get his medication back on track, because he had not yet seen the psychiatrist. According to the autopsy report, and my own eyewitness there was some damage to his eye. They told me he tried to pluck his eye out. There were also abrasions on his back. Something had gone awry, and the autopsy is clear evidence of that. So much so that I felt the need to put it in this book so you can see for yourself. Before Ronald was taken to the prison infirmary on the night he went into a trance, I called the guards for an emergency. I sensed maybe Ronald's medicine was off. They should have taken him to the emergency room if they were not going to take him to the psychiatric hospital. In the autopsy the coroner not only marked two reasons for death [which is a no-no according to the form instructions] but he tried to say that Ronald's place of death was Calloway County Hospital in Fulton, Missouri. This is twenty minutes away from the prison where Ronald died at. The reason I know this is before I know of Ronald's death the Lord spoke a word to me and said I had to forgive. I asked Him, "Forgive what?" A few minutes later two inmates came up to me and said,

"Man, two guards just strangled your brother to death! And we are fixing to riot and tear this place up. We are waiting on you to give us the word!"

I told them, "No, we are not going to do that! Not in my family's name! We are going to wait for an investigation to be done to find out what happened." It wasn't long that the administration sent guards to put me in the hole, because they didn't know how I was going to respond to the death of my brother. This proved to me the incident happened at the prison.

"...riot is the language of the unheard..."
Dr. Martin Luther King Jr.

When someone dies under suspicious circumstances, no one can move the body until the coroner gets there to determine the time of death. I understand why the prison would want to get Ronald's body away from there and to Calloway Community Hospital because from the beginning they didn't do what was right. If there weren't any beds at the Psychiatric Hospital he needed to be at the emergency room until his medication was stabilized. It appears to me, that the doctor who did the autopsy report made it look like they are hiding something. My question is, were the inmates right that two guards strangled him to death and the prison was trying to cover up and protect the guards? They never approached me on the investigation as they should have. The authorities never knew I stopped the talk of rioting. It wasn't until years later that I got a copy of the autopsy report because they had my brother's file sealed for some unknown reason.

If it wasn't for the Chaplin and the in-house psychiatrist who are the ones that are responsible for me getting out of the hole. No telling how long the administration would have kept me locked up there while it appears they were covering up Ronald's death. If it was an accident, why would the coroner stipulate that the cause of death be both natural and accidental? If it is murder, there is no statute of limitation and there needs to be an investigation. Maybe this is the reason that the state will go to any length to cover up a wrongful conviction on one brother and wrongful death on another.

By the way when the Lord spoke to me and said that, "I had to forgive." He also said sometime later, "They won't get away with murder." One of the guards that I was told had something to do with the strangulation would come by my cell and stare in at me when I wasn't looking as though he was feeling guilty, according to my cellmate. The other guard involved in the incident had a family member get charged with pedophilia which was devastating to him. I'm not sure, but I do know the Word teaches us that "*whatever a man soweth that also shall he reap.*" Paul once said sometimes judgment comes before and sometimes it comes after. I remember one time the Lord told me about the state putting me in prison wrongfully, He said, "Sometimes I deal with people in the by and by, but I am going to deal with them in the nigh and nigh."

> "*When they were but a few men in number; yea, very few, and strangers in it. When they went from one nation to another, from one kingdom to another people; He suffered no man to do them wrong: yea, he reproved kings for their sakes; Saying, Touch not mine anointed, and do my prophets no harm. Moreover he called for a famine upon the land: he brake the whole staff of bread.*" (Psalms 105 12-16)

FILED JUL 24 1992

MISSOURI DEPARTMENT OF HEALTH
CERTIFICATE OF DEATH

STATE FILE NUMBER

REGISTRATION DISTRICT NO. 027   REGISTRAR'S NUMBER 75   124- 92 016060

DECEDENT

1 DECEDENT'S NAME (First, Middle, Last)		2 SEX	3 DATE OF DEATH (Month, Day, Year)
RONALD OLIVER, SR.		MALE	JULY 9, 1992

4 SOCIAL SECURITY NO.	5a AGE-Last Birthday (Years)	5b UNDER 1 YEAR	5c UNDER 1 DAY	6 DATE OF BIRTH (Month, Day, Year)	7 BIRTHPLACE (City and State or Foreign Country)
	32			March 1, 1960	St. Louis, MO

8 WAS DECEDENT EVER IN U.S. ARMED FORCES? ☐ Yes ☒ No ☐ Unk

9a PLACE OF DEATH (check only one, see instructions on other side)
HOSPITAL: ☐ Inpatient ☒ ER/Outpatient ☐ DOA OTHER: ☐ Nursing Home ☐ Residence ☐ Other (specify)

9b FACILITY NAME (If not institution, give street and number)	9c CITY, TOWN, OR LOCATION OF DEATH	9d COUNTY OF DEATH
Callaway Community Hospital	Fulton	Callaway

10 MARITAL STATUS - Married, Never Married, Widowed, Divorced (Specify)	11 SURVIVING SPOUSE'S NAME (If wife, give full maiden name)	12a DECEDENT'S USUAL OCCUPATION (Give kind of work done during most of working life. Do not use retired)	12b KIND OF BUSINESS OR INDUSTRY
Widowed	none	Student	College

13a RESIDENCE - STATE	13b COUNTY	13c CITY, TOWN, OR LOCATION	13d ZIP CODE
Missouri	N/A	St. Louis	63136

13e STREET AND NUMBER	13f INSIDE CITY LIMITS	13g YEARS AT PRESENT ADDRESS
10188 Count Dr.	☒ Yes ☐ No	☒ Under 5 ☐ 5-9 ☐ 10-19 ☐ 20 or more

14 WAS DECEDENT OF HISPANIC ORIGIN? (Specify No or Yes - If yes, specify Cuban, Mexican, Puerto Rican, etc.)	15 RACE - American Indian, Black, White, etc. (Specify)	16 DECEDENT'S EDUCATION (Specify only highest grade completed)
☒ No ☐ Yes Specify	Black	Elementary/Secondary (0-12) 12 College (1-4 or 5+) 4+

PARENTS

17 FATHER'S NAME (First, Middle, Last)	18 MOTHER'S NAME (First, Middle, Maiden Surname)
Columbus Oliver	Leanna Harris

INFORMANT

19a INFORMANT'S NAME (Type/Print)	19b MAILING ADDRESS (Street and Number or Rural Route Number, City or Town, State, Zip Code)
Leanna Oliver	10188 Count Dr. St. Louis, MO 63136

DISPOSITION

20a BURIAL, CREMATION, OTHER (Specify)	20b DATE OF DISPOSITION (Month, Day, Year)	20c PLACE OF DISPOSITION (Name of cemetery, crematory, or other place)	20d LOCATION - City or Town, State
Burial	July 15, 1992	Frieden Cemetery	St. Louis, MO

21 SIGNATURE OF FUNERAL SERVICE LICENSEE OR PERSON ACTING AS SUCH	22 NAME AND ADDRESS OF FACILITY	23 FUNERAL ESTABLISHMENT LICENSE NUMBER
► Susi J. James	Whitfield-James Mortuary St. Louis, MO	1201

CAUSE OF DEATH

24 PART I. Enter the diseases, injuries, or complications that caused the death. Do not enter the mode of dying, such as cardiac or respiratory arrest, shock, or heart failure. List only one cause on each line.

		Approximate interval between Onset and Death
IMMEDIATE CAUSE (Final disease or condition resulting in death) ► a.	Bilateral Pulmonary Thromboemboli	
DUE TO (OR AS A CONSEQUENCE OF): b.	Restrained in Bed	
Sequentially list conditions, if any, leading to immediate cause. Enter UNDERLYING CAUSE (disease or injury that initiated events resulting in death) LAST. DUE TO (OR AS A CONSEQUENCE OF): c.		
DUE TO (OR AS A CONSEQUENCE OF): d.		

PART II. Other significant conditions contributing to death but not resulting in the underlying cause given in Part I.

24 IF DECEASED WAS FEMALE 10-49 WAS SHE PREGNANT IN THE LAST 90 DAYS?	25a WAS AN AUTOPSY PERFORMED?	25b WERE AUTOPSY FINDINGS AVAILABLE PRIOR TO COMPLETION OF CAUSE OF DEATH?
☐ Yes ☐ No ☐ Unk	☒ Yes ☐ No	☒ Yes ☐ No

26 MANNER OF DEATH	27a DATE OF INJURY (Month, Day, Year)	27b TIME OF INJURY	27c WAS INJURY ALCOHOL RELATED? (Answer yes or no)	27d INJURY AT WORK?	27e DESCRIBE HOW INJURY OCCURRED
☒ Natural ☐ Pending Investigation ☐ Accident ☐ Suicide ☐ Could not be Determined ☐ Homicide		M	☐ Yes ☐ No ☐ Unk	☐ Yes ☐ No ☐ Unk	
26a (Specify)	27f PLACE OF INJURY - at home, farm, street, factory, office building, etc. (Specify)		27g LOCATION (Street and Number or Rural Route Number, City or Town, State)		

CERTIFIER

28 To the best of my knowledge, death occurred at the time, date and place and due to the cause(s) stated	28a DATE SIGNED (Month, Day, Year)	28b TIME OF DEATH
☐ CERTIFYING PHYSICIAN ☒ MEDICAL EXAMINER/CORONER (Signature and Title) ► Jay Dix md	7-17-92	8:54 A M

29a NAME AND ADDRESS OF CERTIFIER (PHYSICIAN, MEDICAL EXAMINER OR CORONER) (Type or Print)	29b MO LICENSE NUMBER	30 WAS CASE REFERRED TO MEDICAL EXAMINER/CORONER?
Jay Dix, M.D., M.E. Columbia, MO	R9307	☒ Yes ☐ No

31 NAME OF ATTENDING PHYSICIAN IF OTHER THAN CERTIFIER (Type or Print)	32 REGISTRAR'S SIGNATURE	33 DATE RECEIVED BY LOCAL REGISTRAR (Month, Day, Year)
	► Georgia Herron by Shirley Foster, dep	July 21, 1992

CHAPTER 9
Potosi Correctional Center
by
Gregory

There was a season when all over the country they were building for-profit prisons and politicians and investors seized the opportunity to make money. These prisons began to show up on the stock market. It just so happened they built Potosi Correctional Center in Missouri as a maximum-security prison. It is where they decided to move all death row inmates along with what they considered to be the worst of the worst inmates. They moved them all from MSP to Potosi. The worst of the worst was determined by their sentencing. I was given a life sentence running wild with a life sentence without the possibility of probation or parole. Therefore, I was considered one of the worst of the worst.

They bussed us down to Potosi just before I knew Bonnie was coming for a visit and there was no way I could get in touch with her to let her know. She found out when she got to MSP and they told her I was not there. They gave her directions to Potosi and she arrived late in the day, therefore we did not have much time to visit. Potosi was a state-of-the-art prison and exceptionally clean because it was new. There was however an outbreak of lice in the prison, and it got into nearly all the cells. The authorities went through all the cells checking for lice. When they got to our cell, they found no signs of lice. I knew the Lord had covered us as he had covered the Israelites during the plagues and the Passover. Even though Potosi was a new prison there was a tremendous oppressive spirit over the entire campus.

One time when Bonnie came for a visit, she told me as soon as she drove into the parking lot that she could feel the heaviness around the prison. It was so bad she felt like she was being weighed down. When she got inside it was even worse. There was only one woman in the visitors' check-in area and she was sitting with an official at the prison. It was all she could do to continue her descent to the visiting area. After she told me about her experience, I realized that what her spirit was witnessing to her about was the execution that was going to take place that day at midnight. It was the first execution held at Potosi. The warden of Potosi was a Viet Nam veteran and is quoted as commenting about his feelings about the death penalty, "somebody has to take out the trash!" Maybe he was trying to impress the news media with how tough he was on crime. I don't know. Regardless I was not happy with the statement because no matter how one looked at it. He was not the one to judge God's creation in such a demeaning way. It was true, many of those men had done some very heinous crimes against the community but they still were God's creation.

The next day the superintendent came by my cell and started talking to me about the new law that was coming to reduce the stiff sentences and that he was pushing for it to go through because some of you men need a chance to go free. I felt that was the Lord's way of letting me know that this hard-hearted man could even be reached by God.

Every time an execution took place an eerie feeling came over the prison. I along with many others would spend time praying. The staff, guards, and even the chaplain threw a cookie and coffee party before the execution. It was almost as though they were celebrating the ending of an inmate's life.

One of my Christian brothers was on death row and a very strong believer even though he had killed someone. I truly believe he had repented of his sins. We claimed God's deliverance despite the impossibilities for some of the cases. As many men mocked and jeered our stance of faith, we continued to believe in God's promise of setting the captives free. Many of the inmates just could not see God's possibilities of deliverance because their focus was on the electrified fence that was built all around the prison to keep the inmates from escaping.

I knew we had to maintain our stance of faith not only to help our sanity as well to keep hope even when it looked like there wasn't any hope. It went on day in and day out and sometimes even some of the ministers came in and preached against God's power to deliver. We just continued to encourage ourselves in the lord and refused to let any negativity affect our faith.

"And he did not many mighty works there because of their unbelief." (Matthew 13:58)

Potosi Correctional Center

When they moved us to Potosi, they moved 70 'death row' inmates and integrated the death row inmates with the lifers. At that time, they stopped using the expression 'death row inmates' and started calling those inmates 'capital punishment prisoners.' This is one of those semantic games the intellectuals play with words. They could play those games now that they were profiteering from the prisons. Just like they stopped calling them prisons and started calling them Correctional Centers after they took away any of the educational programs from the prisons. Whether you call them 'Death Row' or 'Capital Punishment' inmates it doesn't matter they are still slated for execution by the state. Between 1989 and 2005 there were 62 executions held at Potosi. It was during this integration that I met and became close friends with Darrell Mease the man that believed that the Lord was going to deliver him from 'death row' [Capital Punishment Row?]. Therefore, together we took a stance as examples to other men that God was going to bring us out.

Many men mocked and jeered our stance of faith because of the type of sentence we had. Little did they understand that God was working behind the scenes. It wasn't long, even though the administration's intentions of integrating the 'capital punishment prisoners with the lifers, 80 of us were delivered out of Potosi to JCCC which used to be the old MSP. I took this as a modern-day exodus. They renamed MSP because they were building another new for-profit prison in Jefferson City that would be named Jefferson City Correctional Center. It was at this point that I was walking through the prison yard and ran into an inmate that knew both Darrell and I along with the stance that we took about being delivered. He began to mock and criticize me and said, "you believed that you and Darrell were going to walk out, and they are going to execute Darrell tonight according to the news reports."

I immediately said, "I rebuke that in the name of Jesus!"

It just so happened, that day, Pope John Paul II was visiting St. Louis, Missouri, and stopped in to see the governor and in God's providence, he asked the governor not to execute that man tonight. The governor replied and said, "It was like an epiphany!" He gave Darrell a stay of execution and to this day he was not executed as that mocking inmate thought he would be.

✟

When I was younger, I had a brother that used to tell me, "never fight when you are angry, because it blinds you from thinking straight. There is nothing wrong with walking away and coming back to fight another day." Our fight of faith was a series of battles of fighting the unbelief of people, things, as well as old ideas and doctrines that would have stolen not only the chance for freedom, but as Darrell used to say, "it was a fight for his life!" The old fictional character, Superman had enough sense to know that kryptonite from the planet of Krypton was a threat to him and his strength and he had to stay away from it. So, we as believers must stay away from unbelief so that we can be "walking free." There are so many examples in the Bible where the disciples and Jesus fought the good fight of faith to keep unbelief at bay. An Example; of Jesus keeping unbelief at bay:

Jesus Raises a Dead Girl & Heals a Sick Woman

"And when Jesus was passed over again by ship unto the other side, much people gathered unto him: and he was nigh unto the sea. And, behold, there cometh one of the rulers of the synagogue, Jairus by name; and when he saw him, he fell at his feet, And besought him greatly, saying, My little daughter lieth at the point of death: I pray thee, come and lay thy hands on her, that she may be healed; and she shall live. And Jesus went with him; and many people followed him, and thronged him. And a certain woman, which had an issue of blood twelve years, And had suffered many things of many physicians, and had spent all that she had, and was nothing bettered, but rather grew worse, When she had heard of Jesus, came in the press behind, and touched his garment. For she said, If I may touch but his clothes, I shall be whole. And straightway the fountain of her blood was dried up; and she felt in her body that she was healed of that plague. And Jesus, immediately knowing in himself that virtue had gone out of him, turned him about in the press, and said, Who touched my clothes? And his disciples said unto

him, Thou seest the multitude thronging thee, and sayest thou, Who touched me? And he looked round about to see her that had done this thing. But the woman fearing and trembling, knowing what was done in her, came and fell down before him, and told him all the truth. And he said unto her, Daughter, thy faith hath made thee whole; go in peace, and be whole of thy plague. While he yet spake, there came from the ruler of the synagogue's house certain which said, Thy daughter is dead: why troublest thou the Master any further? As soon as Jesus heard the word that was spoken, he saith unto the ruler of the synagogue, Be not afraid, only believe. And he suffered no man to follow him, save Peter, and James, and John the brother of James. And he cometh to the house of the ruler of the synagogue, and seeth the tumult, and them that wept and wailed greatly. And when he was come in, he saith unto them, Why make ye this ado, and weep? The damsel is not dead, but sleepeth. And they laughed him to scorn. But when he had put them all out, he taketh the father and the mother of the damsel, and them that were with him, and entereth in where the damsel was lying. And he took the damsel by the hand, and said unto her, Talitha cumi; which is, being interpreted, Damsel, I say unto thee, arise. And straightway the damsel arose, and walked; for she was of the age of twelve years. And they were astonished with a great astonishment. And he charged them straitly that no man should know it; and commanded that something should be given her to eat." (Mark 5:21-43 KJV)

"If I Could but Touch"
Drawn by
Bonnie Oliver

Paul said in Timothy 6;12; *Fight the good fight of faith, lay hold on eternal life, whereunto thou art also called, and hast professed a good profession before many witnesses.*

Where there is unbelief even Jesus could not do what he wanted to in his hometown because; *"And he did not many mighty works there because of their unbelief."* (Matthew 13:58)

CHAPTER 10
Behind County Bars
by
Bonnie

During the first week in February 1990, I was researching Martin Luther King Jr. for my Integrative Paper. In his book I Have a Dream, I saw a picture of Dr. King being arrested in Birmingham, Alabama, and being roughed up by white police officers. That picture drew my spirit toward it again and again. The editors quoted Dr. King as saying, "*A man who does not have something for which he is willing to die is not fit to live.*"

Those words kept ringing in my mind, and I knew that we as Christians must have that same commitment toward God. We must be willing to lay our lives on the line for God and His righteousness, justice, and mercy. We can only do that if we have a relationship with Him as our personal God. As these insights developed within my spirit, I felt the Holy Spirit was telling me I, too, would be called upon to suffer arrest and would spend time in jail for the sake of God's justice.

That same night my neighbors upstairs asked me to come up to see a video. The movie was the story of Stephen (Tseombo) Beco, the South African civil rights leader who was arrested and beaten to death for his stand against injustice. When I got home, my spirit was very heavy and upset. I knew beyond any shadow of a doubt that God was confirming what I knew in my heart...He had been speaking to me telling me that I had to go to jail for justice's sake.

I had known for a time (in sketchy detail) that God was calling me to minister to ex-convicts and "an oppressed people." I wrestled with this and shed many tears because of the faith and strength I knew would be required of me. But I kept coming back to the same conclusion: God had called me to the front lines, and He was going to use me in setting the captives free spiritually. I knew life was not going to be easy on the front lines, but I also knew God would equip me for whatever battles lay ahead. And I "knew that I knew: this was from God because I received one confirmation after another.

At the end of February, a couple of weeks before Gregory's appeal hearing, his lawyer sent me a copy of her original brief, the State Attorney's rebuttal, and her counter-brief to his rebuttal. I was angered by the State Attorney's brief but didn't feel at liberty to write anything to the court at that time. In my opinion, the State Attorney's brief was a joke, seeing he did not address any of the pertinent information proving or disproving Gregory's guilt. The state attorney just nit-picked at technicalities about timing issues that were the fault of Gregory's previous Public Defender, a man that Gregory met or only talked to briefly.

As I went about my research for my Integrative paper, I uncovered information that was pertinent to Gregory's case. I prayed about it, then pulled out the briefs and began to pick them apart, based on the Federal "Speedy Trial Act." By the time I got finished, I had built a strong case on Gregory's behalf. I wrote a letter to the Appeals Court addressing the issues of timeliness in Gregory's case...the same things the State Attorney had addressed, only my arguments were against the State. I prayed hard about it and sent the letter to the head judge. I believed God directed me to have it to the court by Wednesday, March 8, 1990, one week prior to Gregory's hearing. That would give the letter time to circulate.

The morning I left to attend Gregory's appeal hearing; I received a phone call from a friend of mine who has a prophetic call in her life. She asked me how much fasting I had done, and I told her which days and which meals that week I had fasted. She told me she thought I had some more coming, so I prayed about it, and I received confirmation. This last fast before the appeal hearing was to be no water or food. Then she gave me several short words from the Lord; the first one being that God had anointed me for the warfare. I was to walk a straight line; God's Spirit was on every man; I was not to lean on my own understanding; I was to praise and pray; I was to anoint the courtroom with oil; I was to heed God's words; God called me out to set the captives free; God was warning me to keep myself pure for the power that was needed. She also gave me some Scripture references, including Hebrews 6:10 and 10:17.

"God is not unjust; he will not forget your work and the love you have shown him as you have helped his people and continue to help them." Hebrews 6:10

"And their sins and iniquities will I remember no more." Hebrews 10:17

On the drive to the hearing, I prayed hard and fasted until 4:00 P.M. as directed. I had also felt directed by God to call a girlfriend of mine to see if I could stay with her while I was in town. After 4:00 P.M., I ate, then drove to meet my girlfriend. I had to go without food and water until after the hearing the next day.

The next morning, March 15, 1990, I arrived at the Court of Appeals at 8:00 A.M. and was shown into the hearing room.

I was reading my Bible when Ms. Lindsey, Gregory's lawyer, came into the room and sat right in front of me. She sat there for a few minutes; then, suddenly, she turned and asked, "Are you Bonnie Stuck?" We talked a little, and she shared with me what she was going to argue that day. Our conversation was cut short when the judges entered the room...the hearing began. State of Missouri v. Oliver was the last case heard.

Ms. Lindsey approached the lectern and began her appeal. During this time, Judge Simeone, the judge I knew was going to be difficult acknowledged that Gregory did not shoot anyone, and he agreed with Ms. Lindsay's assessment that the acceptance of the jury's guilty verdict needed to be reevaluated.

At the end of Ms. Lindsay's argument, Judge Simeone asked abruptly, "Who is Bonnie Lou Stuck?" Ms. Lindsey surprised, pointed me out to him as I raised my hand in the back of the courtroom. "What is she doing writing the court?" he asked gruffly. Ms. Lindsey appeared shocked and uncomfortable at his tone. He questioned, "Did you put her up to this?"

"No, your honor." She replied in a concerned voice.

"Is she a lawyer?"

"No, your honor," Ms. Lindsey answered. "She's a divinity student."

He explained that the last letter I wrote had been sent down to the court. "Doesn't she know she can't write letters to the court?" he asked, still very gruff.

After Ms. Lindsay's and my brief discussion, I drove down to Potosi Prison, about 65 miles away, to see Gregory.

As I entered the building, the guard acted as though she recognized me from my last visit, six months before.

"Oh, yes who is it you want to visit again?"

"Gregory Oliver."

She handed me an information card and asked me to fill it out for file updating, so I did. Gregory had been transferred to this new "super-max" facility in Potosi because of the length of his sentence. It was from that card that a new computer check was done on my record.

Six hours after the court adjourned, while I was visiting with Greg, I was asked by one of the guards to go up to the front desk. I knew, in my spirit, this was it. I was in trouble. Judge Simeone had appeared angry with me at the hearing. I was expecting to get arrested for the letters I had written.

When I saw the Sheriff's Deputy, I wasn't sure the extent of my trouble. The guard at the desk abruptly told me to sign out. I did so without arguing. The Sheriff's Deputy went through his procedure asking my name, etc.

Then he said, "I have a warrant for your arrest."

"For what?" I asked.

"For a dog running at large in 1986."

"You've got to be kidding," I laughed.

"No, ma'am, I'm not. The O'Fallon Police are on their way here to get you."

I couldn't figure out how in the world there could be a warrant for my arrest that was supposedly issued on April 1, 1986, when I had been cleared to visit the Missouri State Penitentiary twice in 1987, and again in 1988. Also in 1988, I was cleared to visit another State Penitentiary. Then in July 1988, I was stopped and ticketed for expired tags on a rental car I was driving while my car was in the shop. And in early 1989, I was stopped (not ticketed) in Illinois for wearing earphones while driving. Because I had a Missouri driver's license, the officer had to run a check on the Joint States' list of warrants. None of these computer checks had shown any warrant for my arrest. Suddenly, four years later the very same day a judge gets indignant about my writing letters to the court, I was being arrested on a trumped-up charge for something I had no knowledge of until that day.

After I was arrested, the officer took me to the local jail. I was booked and mug shots were taken. The sign I held up in front of my mug shot read,

Bonnie Lou Stuck
Dog at Large
March 15, 1990

I was now one of the bad guys, but not only that—I was a "dog at large," which I find quite humorous. I would love to see a picture of that mug shot.

I was put in a holding area that had a one-piece unit lavatory and stool. There was a brick wall divider that had a shower behind it, and the entire room was 14'10" long and 6' wide. There was a wooden slat bench about 8' long. The door was heavy metal with one 8" by 8" window, which was covered with paper. The room was cold, and I was wearing a lightweight summer dress. At least the guard let me take my Bible and a pen in the cell area.

I felt the peace of the Lord through the whole ordeal and was not upset or panicky. I was to wait for the O'Fallon Police to come to take me back to O'Fallon, over 100 miles away. It was my understanding that the police do not drive over 25 miles from their base to pick anyone up unless it is a wanted felon. I don't think I fell into that category!

After a couple of hours, the guard moved me to another cell, which was much smaller and had no facilities. It was the "drunk tank," and it was stripped of everything. The floor was the only place to sit. The guard did, however, give me a chair to sit on, which I appreciated. I continued to read my Bible, and God showed me a couple of Scriptures. I found myself reading the Psalms, which I seldom read. The Spirit began to minister to me as I began to read Psalms 105:13-15:

"When they went from one nation [State] to another
From one kingdom [freedom] to another people [prisoner],
He permitted no one to do them wrong;
Yes, He rebuked kings [judges] for their sakes,
Saying, "Do not touch My anointed ones,
And do My prophets no harm." (NKJV)

Those verses ministered to me and I was reminded of another time when I was anointed for the Lord's work, and people who came out against me were punished severely.

The second verse of Scripture that quickened my spirit was 1 Peter 2:13:

"Therefore submit yourselves to every ordinance of man for the Lord's sake, whether to the king as supreme, or to governors, as to those who are sent by him for the punishment of evildoers and for the praise of those who do good. For this is the will of God that by doing good you may put to silence the ignorance of foolish men as free, yet not using liberty as a cloak for vice, but as bondservants of God." (NKJV)

I knew that the peace I was feeling was giving me the strength not to get angry at the stupidity of the whole situation. I knew, too, that my behavior commanded the respect of the guards because they treated me like a lady. You could tell the sheriff's deputy refrained from laughing at the whole situation. He stated under his breath as he shook his head,

"We have all kinds of dogs running around this county." The police had a job to do; I didn't fault them for it.

I had spent a couple of hours in the small drunk tank and was uncomfortable because I had to relieve myself. In my mind, I let God know my discomfort and, suddenly, the guard opened the cell and took me back to the other cell, which was larger, warmer, and had facilities. During this time, I began singing praise to the Lord, and He gave me some beautiful words that I sang out loud. I knew that God was in control and that He would find Himself glorified by this experience–somehow.

The O'Fallon Police finally arrived, and I was let out. I still hadn't made my phone call, so I asked if I could call before we left. I knew we had a two-hour drive ahead of us. I was allowed to call my sister and then I was ready to go. The sergeant who was driving pulled out his handcuffs and just sort of looked at me, bewildered and almost embarrassed at the situation.

"I'm going to cuff you in front."

"Aren't you required to cuff women in front?" I asked.

"No, we aren't."

I held my hands out, and he gently placed the cuffs on me. He took extra precaution not to cut off the circulation to my hands.

Once at the O'Fallon Police Station, I had to go through another booking process, this time including fingerprinting. When everything was done and they were getting the paperwork together, the police officer on inside duty said, "Bonnie, there's no paperwork here to indicate you were ever notified of the complaint with a summons."

"You're right," I said. "I had no idea. If I had, I would have taken care of it four years ago."

That was sufficient proof to me that this was a clear case of harassment to try to scare me off whatever God was leading me to do regarding Gregory's case. My letters would not threaten any person who had integrity.

I could not legally be prevented from helping Gregory, therefore something from the past had to be used against me, no matter how stupid or insignificant. The "dog-at-large" complaint was the only thing that could have caused this incident to occur. It must have laid dormant all this time because the police knew the reputation of the neighbor who made the complaint. He called the police for everything, including me watering the grass, in his opinion, too much. This warrant materialized because somebody wanted to find a way to interfere with what I was doing in Gregory's case.

On March 22, 1990, I received, in the mail, a summons dated March 16, 1990, from the City of O'Fallon. The summons was for a "dog-at-large," for which I was arrested on March 15, 1990. This was evidence proving I had never been served a summons four years prior and that I was arrested unjustly, and that Gregory's case was a case of fraudulent concealment.

By the end of March, I received a letter from the Public Defender's Office about the Appeal Hearing where the judge struck out at me over my letter writing. The judge's outburst upset Gregory's Attorney too, so she went back to her office and checked to make sure that she did nothing wrong in sending me both sides of the argument prior to the hearing. The enclosed letter is proof the judge [the mentor of the trial judge] errored when striking out at me over my letter writing to the court.

The following letter is the letter Bonnie wrote to the Appeal Court that caused Judge Simeone to strike out at her in court because of her letter writing. This judge was the mentor of the trial judge who brushed aside the erroneous verdict that should have been a mistrial. Six hours later Bonnie was arrested on a trumped-up charge and spent six hours in jail, three of which was in the drunk tank all because of the illegalities the court did not want to be exposed. She was also transported over 100 miles handcuffed...all for a 'Dog off a leash' from 1986.

March 3, 1990
Court of Appeals
 St. Louis, MO

Ref: Gregory Oliver's appeal

Dear Judge, Pudlowski
    I didn't think I would be writing the court again, but I had the opportunity to read the briefs that Ms. Green, Attorney for the defense, and the Attorney General's office put together for this appeal hearing. I must say Judge, Ms. Green did a very good job in putting the case together while the Attorney General's office is doing nothing but drawing at straws. On top of reading the briefs, I found some interesting information while working on my major research paper at school. I happened to run into information, laws and regulations that I believe can apply to this case and show an area in which the defendant was definitely prejudiced at his trial. This is in addition to the areas that have been brought out in lawyers briefs., for both the 29-15 and the appeal. I will try and make this brief.
    1. I noticed that the Attorney General's office did not address any of the issues that Ms. Green brought out in her brief, which were pertinent to the case. They only address technicalities that were not pertinent to Mr. Oliver's defense. Technicalities that did not touch on whether he was guilty or not, or

whether he received a fair trial. He did not even back up the erroneous charges brought against Mr. Oliver by Mr. Randall during the trial

2. I feel [there is a contradiction] based on the information Ms. Green supplied on the inefficiency of the system, prior to Mr. Oliver's hearing. The fact that your state did not hold to the dates brings up some real critical areas that were overlooked in the past as well. If the Attorney General's office is able to draw at straws after the fact, then I think it is necessary that all the straws be pulled out of the container as well. I will refer to some important Federal rulings I discovered in my other research. The following information was obtained from the Bureau of Justice, Department of Statistics 1988.

A. Baker v. Wingo (1972) The "U.S. Supreme Court set down four factors to be weighted in determining whether a defendant had been denied the right to a speedy trial:
   o Length of the delay
   o Reason for the delay
   o Whether the defendant was responsible for the delay.
   o Whether delay prejudiced the case of the defendant.

B. Most criminal cases are disposed of in six months or less, except in chronically delayed State courts. Missouri was not listed; therefore, I could only assume that it must be a chronic case.

C. Missouri has a 190-day speedy trial restriction for defendants not in custody. That 190-day time is just under seven months.

D. Cases, however, resulting in trials generally take longer than ones that end in dismissals or guilty pleas. They average more than seven months which equals 210 days.

E. The Federal Speedy Trial Act of 1974, amended in 1979, specifies time standards for each stage in the

Federal court process. Thirty days are allowed from arrest to filing of an indictment or information; 70 days are allowed between information or indictment and trial. Certain time periods, which as defense-requested continuances, are not counted. If case processing time exceeds the limit, the case may be dismissed.

F. I will now attempt to recap Mr. Oliver's case for you to show you that the nit picking of the Attorney General's office needs to consider all the information and realize that Mr. Oliver's case went beyond the limits of acceptable for many reasons. Was it really necessary for the courts to find Mr. Oliver guilty because of the numerous delays which cause the process to wind up being three times longer than acceptable? According to the way that I read and understand the situation, Mr. Oliver's case would have been dismissed because of the inefficiency of the courts and public defender's office. The problem falls upon the State 100%. Draw your attention the hearing transcripts for the 29-15 page 70. Mr. Knappenberger says that he was not called on the case until January 1987. Prior to that time Mr. Oliver's case was in the Public Defender's office. Therefore, of the twenty-two months it took for this case to come to a speedy trial, it was only in the hands of private defense counsel for three months.

ACTION: CRITICAL TIMES	DAYS
Time from arrest to filing. "Speedy Trial Act (STA)	30
Information indictment and trial STA (not counting continuances) STA_____	70_
 Total days allowed by Federal Gov't (not counting continuances)	100

Missouri 1968 restrictions for non-incarcerated defendants 190 days: Equals (3-30 day continuances)	190
Mr. Oliver arrested June, 1985. Mr. Oliver's trial April, 1987 Time waiting for trial	600
Number of days non-incarcerated defendants wait because of state restrictions	$\leq$190 $\geq$
Wasted days equals 13.67, different 30-day continuances	
Grand Total of wasted days violating "Speedy Trial Act"	410

The last point is only speculation as to the number of continuances, but I have a copy of the case record from the original filing of the appeal to the last date given for the brief to be submitted which was 11/20/1989. There was, however, another extension after the filing dates. I am aware that the appeal was held up due to the record in a period of 13 months there was a total of seven extensions: five by the Public Defender's Office and two by the Attorney General's office. If this is true for that thirteen-month period while being handled by the State Public Defender's office, what happened for seventeen months prior to the trial and the obtaining of private lawyers? To my knowledge the Public Defender's office only saw Mr. Oliver once in seventeen months and that was for a short period of time. One visit in seventeen months does not constitute any form of professionalism. Yet the Sixth amendment of the Constitution provides the accused the right to be assisted by counsel....

One more point proving the excessive length of time violating the "Speedy Trial Act." On page 7 and 8 of the trial transcripts, [the pre-trial hearing] Mr. Randall, attorney for the State, reminded the court about the length of time that Mr. Oliver's case had been pending.

> Mr. Randall: "Your Honor, I think this is the oldest case in the entire Circuit, short of Appellate Court reversals.... The case has just been delayed over and over again. I don't see that there's any, justice would be served in any manner by further delaying it, especially at this point."

Mind you the private lawyers had only been on the case three months and the Public Defender's office was sleeping on this case or did not want to tackle it. Justice could have been better served if the lawyers had more than three months to prepare for what wound up to be an eight-day jury trial. Notice Mr. Randall said, "...especially at this point." Which I believe did nothing more than infer the shakiness of the situation. I also believe that the unusual time involved in this case definitely prejudiced the case. How could the court find him not guilty after keeping him locked up for so long?

Now, I would like to ask, in what aspect can you as reasonable and prudent decision makers say that:

1.	Mr. Oliver is even guilty.
2.	That Mr. Oliver received a fair trial.
3.	That Mr. Oliver is responsible for the gross miscarriage of justice that has fallen upon him. [He trusted the system]
4.	That Mr. Oliver received effective representation, throughout the entire case. Excluding Ms. Green and the work Ms. Kelly did on the 29-15.
5.	That Mr. Oliver was not prejudiced at his trial.
6.	That Mr. Oliver was not affected by the length of the delay mentioned in the Baker v. Wingo (1972) Supreme Court decision.
7.	That Mr. Oliver was not affected by the reasons for the delay and mentioned in Baker v. Wingo (1972) Supreme Court Decision.

Your Honor the list goes on in this case. I would like to believe that this innocent man has the possibility of having his case heard at the appeal level without bias and prejudice. The Attorney General's office is trying to hold to dates that had never been held to before and nothing else.

How is it that a man's future is judged by a couple of dates and not pertinent facts that prove not only his innocence but his lack of knowledge to what his crazy brother was going to do.

If you do accept that information in the Attorney General's brief pertaining to an after-the -fact event as relevant, then I think a look at the "Speedy Trial Act" and a review of Mr. Oliver's case, in reference to the extended time it took for Mr. Oliver's case to come to trial, is necessary because I believe it to be a violation of the "Speedy Trial Act." I ask at this point, "Who is in violation of anything? It is not Mr. Oliver. He is innocent! Again, Your Honor thank you for your attention.

Kindest Regards,
Bonnie Lou Stuck

MISSOURI STATE PUBLIC DEFENDER SYSTEM

APPELLATE/PCR DIVISION - EASTERN DISTRICT
1221 LOCUST STREET, SUITE 410
ST. LOUIS, MISSOURI 63103
(314) 421-1213

March 20, 1990

Ms. Bonnie Stuck
708 Crescent, Apt. 7A
Wheaton, IL 60187

Dear Bonnie:

I was very pleased to meet you last Thursday. I am glad you
came to the oral argument. I just wanted to inform you that
I have asked some attorneys about the Judges' comments
concerning your letter writing. The fact of the matter is
that you have a constitutional (First Amendment) right to
write Judges. Anybody can mail letters.

As an attorney, I have an ethical obligation to write the
clerk of the Court and ask her to forward my letter to the
Judges. I am not supposed to write Judges directly.
However, since you are not an attorney you are free to do as
you please.

I am not sure why the Judges gave me such a difficult time
last Thursday. Perhaps they were impressed with your legal
writing and thought I had told you what to write in the
letter. Maybe in some of your letters you struck a tiny
bone of guilt in a Judge and he does not want the general
public to know about such travesties as Gregory's case.
(This is an unlikely hypothesis - - - the Judges probably
believe Gregory is guilty if the jury found him guilty).

I am not encouraging nor discouraging you from writing the
Judges but I am telling you that neither of us broke any
laws or ethical codes by your writing.

Sincerely,

Assistant Public Defender

KGG/pl

CHAPTER 11
Jefferson City Correctional Center — JCCC
by

Gregory

After a season at Potosi, the administration realized that not everyone with long sentences was the "worst of the worst" and they sent me back to Jefferson City Correctional Center which was temporarily housed in the old Missouri State Penitentiary. They changed the name because they were building a new for-profit prison in the Jefferson City, MO area. For me, it was like a modern-day exodus. There were some changes in the old building when I got back there. The visiting room had been revamped and made bigger. There was no longer a section for those visiting men on death row. I did go back to my original housing unit which was known as the honor dorm.

It was sometime later that I found out that there were 80 of us delivered to JCCC. We were beginning to get settled in. It seemed like Missouri was constructing new for-profit prisons all over the place. The men that continued to mock my faith were relentless and because there is not much for many men to do in prison some of the men made it their new pastime to mock me. They would say things like, "You thought that you would be free by now. The only place you are going is to one of the new prisons."

"I shall not be moved!" I told them. "You can't stop a gone man." I had hung signs and banners up that Bonnie made for me to display in the cell. Saying things like "It's a Done Deal. I'm a Gone Man" and "Out the Door in '94." It was 1994 when my case went to the Governor's Office. At the end of 1994, the Lord spoke a word to me and said now, "*shut the door.*"

Much of what the Lord was directing me to do and say, I did not have a clue what a lot of it meant, but I just had to trust and obey. That way I would leave the outcome up to him.

I remember one time the Lord had me pack my boxes and go up to the Guard's bubble to ask them, "Do you have my release papers?" I did what the Lord said even though it made me look crazy.

Little did I know years later after I was released that gesture of mine would come back as a positive. I was out and I was attending a speaking engagement sharing my testimony. This lady suddenly stopped me from talking and said, "I know you—you are the guy who packed your boxes and asked the guards for your release papers. I know a lot of men might have thought you were off, but my husband told me about you." I told him that he, "better pack his boxes too."

"Praise the Lord, He honored that step of faith many years later.

The day the Lord had me pack my boxes; the staff sent me to the prison psychiatrist. I explained to him how the Lord directed me to take that stand of faith. He then told me that he, too, was a believer and, "I am believing with you. By the way—who sent you over here to me anyway?" He asked.

When the prison population grew to be above capacity, 5200 inmates...way more than it was designed to hold; the state began to transfer a massive number of inmates to the newly built for-profit prisons in the state. Most of the inmates could envision being transferred to one of these prisons and they didn't want to go. They believed that going to these for profits that they will be more of a commodity than men. For example, a friend of ours, husband went to Cameron Correctional Center. What these inmates ran into was a lot of revolting which was causing a lot of time in lockdown with no time out at all. The worst revolt that they had happened on May 12, 2018, when a group of men destroyed the kitchen and again came not only the lockdowns but the transferring of the men to another prison.

Out of fear...many of them started volunteering to be transferred to a prison of their choosing. This was also a time when they were transferring the low-risk inmates to other states guaranteeing them lighter sentences. The television station that Bonnie worked for did a documentary on some of the Missouri men that were transferred to Texas. In the documentary, the video showed the men crawling naked on the ground maneuvering through a path lined with angry guard dogs. Some say it was a training exercise. In another video shots the Missouri men were placed in a cell and big hoses, like the ones firemen use, were turned on them. There seemed to be no escape from the high-pressure hoses. History has a way of repeating itself. In the book of Ecclesiastes it proves this point *"The thing that hath been, it is that which shall be; and that which is done is that which shall be done: and there is no new thing under the sun.* (Ecclesiastes 1:9) What happened in Texas to the Missouri inmates was no different than what Rep. Eugene [Bull] Connor did in Alabama during the Civil Rights Movement. He was known as a staunch segregationists and was known for using police dogs and fire hoses to thwart the Civil Right demonstrations in 1962-1963. This is one of the major problems of the constant warehousing of human beings in our prison systems. All of this is done under the guises of public safety and being tough on crime.

The state of Missouri wound up suing the state of Texas. We thought that even though some of the inmates were compensated somewhat, the state should not have been compensated because they were complicit in sending the inmates there. I understand that the Feds took over the case, but did they sue the state of Missouri? I doubt it. If you or I sent someone into a yard with wild dogs and one of the dogs bit them, we would be liable. How can a state get away with wrongdoing repeatedly?

I remember years ago that a man was placed in prison wrongfully for a minor crime that he didn't do. The state continually pushed him until he broke. They were trying to convict him for a crime he committed in prison, but the Feds took over and officials wound up going to prison. Because the officials were trying to punish him repeatedly, which is not legal. Once a person is legitimately convicted and placed in a prison that is his/her punishment. They can't beat them with rubber hoses, psychologically abuse them, or create other means of punishment that are not sanctioned by the court.

If a person is given the death penalty, that is his punishment until the death warrant is given to execute that person to carry out the court's order. If a person is given a life sentence, that is his punishment until the sentence is carried out. If there is evidence that warrants another look because there are errors in the case, then these judgments and sentences are subject to reversal. Therefore, some cases take a while for certain things to be carried out because man is not infallible.

✝

After most of the men transferred to other prisons, the staff started putting together lists of forced transfers. Some of the men who mocked and jeered my stance would come by the cell and say, "you're on the next bus."

I would tell them, "I shall not be moved." This went on for months and each time the mockers would be shocked that I was still there. I don't know if they were selecting the inmates to leave chronologically or randomly but my name never came upon a list. The movement of men eventually wound down as the need to fill the other prisons waned. Still, my name did not end up on any list. I continued to work in the kitchen and became the top chef and baker. I also continued to go to the library and church events to occupy my time. I didn't' realize that working in the kitchen was going to lead to becoming the top chef, but later, down the road, I found out the reason the Lord was directing me this way. Most of the men wanted to work down in industry because they could make money there. The Lord was teaching me that it is not how much money you make. It seemed that every time I signed up to go down to industry, the Lord would close the door. I just continued to do the best I could do where I was.

✝

I was coming from the recreation yard one day and I heard the Lord speak a word to me, "Watch your back!" There was an urgency with this message. I was walking in a corridor where a lot of stabbings often took place it was known to be a death trap. I started looking around. As soon as I got back to the housing unit, one of the inmates that I played chess with quite often called me over to the side and said, "Hey Big O, I need to talk to you."

"Okay." And we began to talk.

"There are some guys that think you snitched on an inmate named Psycho."

"Snitched on him about what? Who are these guys?"

"Don't worry about it, I know you didn't. I told them you weren't that type of person and that you wouldn't do something like that because you don't mess around in other people's business. Let me do some checking around and see if I can find out what is going on."

I knew that the word the Lord spoke to me was correct and He was warning me ahead of time to stay alert. It is always good to know that the Lord has our back in times of trouble. I really think this was his way of assuring me that nothing can happen beyond His knowledge. It was a few days later that the inmate came back to me and told me. "Don't worry about what I talked to you about the other day. We found out that it was his friends that told on him."

"The thing is that these men did not have the courage to confront me and ask me before making such an allegation." I knew what incident they were talking about because that inmate stabbed a guard who enjoyed harassing inmates. I didn't know who the inmate was because he was in a homemade Ninja suit—everything was covered up. The only people who could have known were those who were close enough to see him put it on. He came from upstairs some place when the incident took place. It was good that the Lord had alerted me because it gave me the chance to pray, and this place was the type of place that a person's life can be on the line at any moment. I thought it was crappy that these men didn't have the ware with all to come and apologize after they found out that it was Psycho's own friends that turned him in.

While I was working in the kitchen, it gave me an opportunity to evangelize. I would take the food cart to the hospital. When I first started going to the hospital, I didn't know what to expect and when I reached the rooms, I would speak to the inmates asking them how they were doing. I noticed that some of them were very sick. They had a double whammy, sickness, and prison, not to mention the depression that was on them. I asked them if I could pray for them and many of them would allow me to. Eventually, I looked forward to going over to the hospital to pray and minister to the men. This went on for quite a while. One day I decided to take the cart over to the hospital and I was excited because I was going to be able to minister to the men over there. To my surprise, the area was totally empty. I wondered, why I was there? They had me come to the hospital to pick up the carts and not to deliver trays of food. I sensed the Lord wanted me to be there for some reason and after being there for a few minutes, I noticed a shelf with books on it. I had remembered hearing a preacher speak about a young man, Keith Green, who had a powerful ministry and how the Lord walked him step by step to accomplish his vision. My eyes quickly glanced at the books, and I noticed this guy's picture and his name, it was Keith Green. The book was "*No Compromise.*" This caught my attention, and I knew I had to read this book, but how in the world would I get a book from the hospital back over to the cell—that is a—no, no. The Lord just told me, "Ask the guard if you can borrow it." So, I did just that. To my surprise, the guard told me to bring it back next week. I knew what I was going to be doing for the next several days in order to get the book back on time. It was an excellent read. What really blessed me the most was parallel to my own promises such as the promises the Lord made him. When I got into the book, I didn't want to put it down. It did encourage me and strengthened my faith. I didn't feel like going over to the hospital that day because I felt it was a waste of time, really the Lord wanted to minister to me, and He did.

One thing for certain, why time can really drag in prison so it is always good to fill your day with something to keep you from being discouraged. I found playing chess was very relaxing, but it depends on who you are playing with. Some of the men are so competitive that it can create a problem sometimes. I ran into that as I was playing chess with a young Muslim guy, and for the most part, we always had some good games. This particular day he was more competitive than usual. I think I had already beaten him a couple of games, but he wanted to keep playing. I ended up winning and he got so angry that he hit me in the jaw. I stood up, and he did not know what to think. I turned to the right I asked him, "Do you want to hit the other side?" He began to tremble and stormed out of the cell angry. A couple of hours later he came back down, and he apologized. You could tell he felt terrible. Then to my surprise, he told me that the Lord told him that he could really trust me. That was very healing to me, and I did forgive him, but I told him I wouldn't play any more chess with him that day. We both laughed.

There was another guy whose cell I liked to go to and talk with a lot, his name was Samuel. I think he liked talking to me too. Seeing I had my Paralegal degree he knew I understood the law. For me, I knew it was an opportunity for me to talk to him about the Lord. Samuel was very bitter for a couple of reasons, 1. Not only for being in prison but 2. His mother had passed of cancer. He turned his back on the Lord and blamed God for it. He gave me a little information about how devoted his mother was to the Lord. I told him "your mom was well and with the Lord, but she would be concerned about you."

He said, "Why?"

"Well, why do you think your mom named you Samuel? Samuel is a prophet's name, and your mom wants you saved."

"Well God took her; how can I trust a God that took her?"

"Samuel, God's ways are not our ways, and we have to understand and trust that He knows what needs to be in your life, your mom's life, or my life. The thing is that your mom had faith even through death, and she will live forever with the Lord. That is what she wants for you."

He wrestled with that then said, "Why hasn't God got you out—you're innocent?"

"Samuel, I am going to walk free."

"Well until I see this it will be hard for me to believe."

It wasn't that long after Samuel and I went through many of these episodes and then finally the day came I was transferred to the Release Center at Algoa. Many of the men came out to wish me well and was surprised at what the Lord had done. I don't know if I saw Samuel that day when I left, but I do know the one guy that mocked Darrell Mease and myself a lot was too heartbroken to see me off. This guy missed out on appreciating two opportunities of witnessing God's magnificent work. Darrell not being executed and me walking out of prison.

When I arrived at Algoa it was months later that one of Samuels friends came to the release center. As soon as he saw me, he ran up to me to tell me the news. I was really concerned about Samuel because not only did he turn his back on the Lord, but He started worshiping Satan and even had a devil's bible. As Samuel's friend approached me, he said, "Guess what Samuel has flushed the devil's bible down the toilet stool and given his life to the Lord all because of you?"

"Oh, no that is all God's doing. I am so happy to hear that even though I didn't get to see it for myself. Thank you for the news." I realized at that point that when the Lord has us plant seeds, He will complete the work even though we are not around.

CHAPTER 12
Even the Feds
The DEA's Corrupt Snitch
by
Gregory & Bonnie

The years continued to pass and the new Missouri governor was losing popularity fast. During the first two years of his administration, he went through five key people, including several Chief Legal Councils so Gregory's case along with over 1,000 others went on hold—more delays. I struggled with these delays, and I was beginning to believe that the truth would never be heard the way Gregory and I knew it needed to be. Gregory's case was wrapped up in so many legal lies that were like a 'Gordian Knot' and began to disguise itself as truth to those who didn't know the real truth. (The Big lie is born "If you tell a **lie big** enough and keep repeating it, people will eventually come to believe it." This Ideology is attributed to Joseph Goebbels...It also appeared in Hitler's *Mein Kampf)* This was not acceptable to either of us. Another quote from a movie that I did not like because it glorified a crooked cop was, "The Training Day." [Sorry Denzel, but I loved The Hurricane and watched it over 30 times.] This quote was proving to be true in Gregory's case. *"It is not what you know but what you can prove!"* Gregory and I knew the truth about the rigging of his case, but how could we prove the truth that we discovered in the transcripts and the case file.

☦

About this time, I lost my job. I was 58 years old. What do you do when you are over-educated and under-qualified? I have a bit of an adventurous spirit, so I went to a truck driving school and Unemployment paid for it. Their condition was that I had to drive for a year, or I would have to pay the schooling back. I began driving for Swift Transportation in 2003 and drove from coast to coast and worked seven days a week many hours a day. Communication with Gregory was almost void during this season. I didn't have a home, just an address in Michigan and Missouri where I could be contacted. Gregory couldn't call me because I only had a cell phone so the only time we could talk was when I visited about once a month, but occasionally that time stretched to once every two months depending on my load assignments. Therefore, we had to exercise extreme faith and trust in each other.

One day when I was going to visit Greg, I felt led to stop by the Probation and Parole Office to see if someone from the clemency board would talk to me. I was able to talk to the new director's secretary, Samantha. She remembered me from my meetings with the previous director. She told me the governor had just appointed another new chief council— so new that she didn't even know his name. That made the fifth chief council since the new governor was sworn in. Then she told me that this administration had hired a consultant to work on all the clemency cases that were on the governor's desk, which was over 1,000 cases at the time. To my astonishment the consultant they hired was Shellie Freund, the woman I had worked the closest with during the previous administration. Again, I was assured that because Gregory's case hadn't been denied that it was a good sign.

In the meantime, we were to wait, but not without the Lord revealing another bit of important information in a remarkable way. Just when we thought we had opened every avenue of deception that took place in Gregory's case more information fell right into our lap. One evening Gregory was playing dominoes with another inmate, Jerry who was in prison for drug dealing. Another inmate, Morris rushed into the cell as though he had seen a ghost and asked Jerry for his album. Gregory had no idea what he was talking about so began to listen. Jerry's album was a collection of articles and pictures of drug snitches. Jerry gave him the album and Morris began looking for an article from the St. Louis Post Dispatch that he had remembered about the highest-paid narcotics snitch. This article confirmed what he just saw on television. The *Discovery Channel* had just aired a show on the Federal Government's highest-paid narcotic's snitch that was working for the DEA. "I have to see if you have this information on this Chambers guy." Gregory's ears perked up! Chambers, he thought, was the name of the stranger who got shot in his case and who the prosecutor 'nolle pros' a first-degree assault case against Gregory and his brother Ronald.

"The Discovery Channel just aired a show on him and said that he was working out of the St. Louis area as a drug snitch," Morris said. Gregory sat there dumbfounded as he listened and watched.

In the album was a newspaper article from the St. Louis Post Dispatch about the corruption in the Federal Government's highest-paid narcotic's snitch, Andrew Chambers. Chambers happened to be from the St. Louis area and was the third victim in the State of Missouri v. Oliver case. Chambers was at the apartment the night of the shooting finding his way around the drug trafficking areas for PCP in St. Louis. Gregory was at this house for 'sex'. Gregory kept telling the authorities that were investigating the scene that they were smoking PCP. He knew this because of the lingering odor in the room. Burning PCP smells a bit like formaldehyde. The article in the scrapbook indicated that Chambers, who started working for the DEA in 1984, was probing for this information in trying to discover the main dealers between St. Louis and California market. Chambers was on the Feds payroll for 16 years and had earned over four million federal dollars.

The use of drugs or the activities in the apartment that night was not allowed to come out at trial because it would challenge the character of the tenants, including the only eyewitness in the apartment. The defense was not allowed to attack the character of any of the state witnesses. Now we knew why...they were protecting the drug snitch, which at the time of the trial was being held in somewhat of a Witness Protection Program. Whenever the DEA felt Chambers was in danger they moved him to protect him, Being shot in the leg was a possible threat to his work with the DEA.

We now knew 'why' they "nolle pros" the first-degree assault against Andrew Chambers when Ronald shot him in the leg. This new information answered nearly all our questions as to 'why the prosecution handled the case the way he did. The prosecutor acknowledged that Gregory hadn't committed any criminal activity in an out-of-jury range discussion to the court and defense. So why did he prosecute if his boss wasn't putting pressure on him because of what Greg's grandfather did? The authorities on several levels were making certain that Chambers and the activities happening at the residence of Diane Moore were kept quiet for their agenda. Consequently, Gregory was the *scapegoat* for not only his brother but for Andrew Chambers' activities with the DEA's investigations as well. Janet Reno, Attorney General under the Clinton Administration at the time, finally barred Chambers' activity with the DEA and forbade them from using him.

As soon as I found all this out, I put together a hand-written presentation and took it directly to the Probation and Parole Office to give it to Samantha. At first, she wondered about Andrew Chambers' connection to the case. I let her know he was the third shooting victim. She assured me that the information would be passed on to the proper people—namely Shellie, who was the woman that I have worked with during the previous administration and who was hired as a consultant to help get the 1,000 clemency cases off the governor's desk before the end of his administration. The governor was not seeking another term. One of the miracles of this whole thing was—they were consulting with all of the people that I had established relationships with from the previous administration.

In Chamber's deposition, for the State of Missouri v. Oliver, he only supported the prosecution's supposition that they were smoking marijuana. He did not offer the truth that it was marijuana laced with PCP his drug of choice and the drug he was undercover for and giving any leads to the Feds. The key thing in his testimony that supported Gregory's testimony was that he said Gregory was hollering at his brother "you can't go shooting people! What is you doing?" This proved that Gregory had no control over Ronald and there was no motive or intent on his part. But the jury was not privy to this information, just as they were not privy to other pertinent facts in the case either. It might have made a difference even though the jury was stacked with relatives of the Ringer hearsay on hearsay witness who was related to the deceased Mr. Campbell and the relatives who were on the jury.

When I think of all the things that we have uncovered in this case it concerned me because the societal good guys are just as guilty if not guiltier of violating a person's constitutional rights to a fair and impartial trial as they are trying to convince the public of the felon's guilt. Their crime is greater because the prosecution concocted a case based on inferential lies passed off as circumstantial evidence. This is what created the legal lies around the state of Missouri v. Oliver case and at each appeal level, the law protected and covered up the lies as well as concocting more lies. It is said that this continues, but it does and will continue Because Judges and Prosecutors have absolute immunity. In 1976 the Supreme Court decided that prosecutors have absolute immunity—and cannot be sued for misconduct related to their activity in the courtroom. They are immune from:

- o   Falsifying evidence
- o   Coercing witnesses
- o   Soliciting and knowingly sponsoring perjured testimony
- o   Withholding exculpatory evidence and /or evidence of innocence
- o   Introducing evidence known to be illegally seized at trial.
- o   Initiating a prosecution in bad faith (in other words, for personal reasons or with the knowledge that the individual didn't commit the crime)

Ref: NAPA The National Police Accountability Project

Based on this list we can see here the prosecutor in Greg's case did every one of these things and in his deposition, he as much as admitted to some of it. This is totally discriminating. This ruling allows the prosecutor to lie, cheat and steal to get a conviction even if he/she knows the defendant is innocent. What is ironic is that prosecutors prosecute people who do this same thing, and they are considered felons. Something that concerns me is that so many of our legislators are former prosecutors. Shouldn't these things be considered illegal? If it is illegal for one it is illegal for all and the minute they do it they are stepping outside the color of their office and should be held accountable. I am sure that is what the framers wanted.

On November 24, 2004, there was a message from my friend Fae that she wanted me to call her at home as soon as possible. When I did, she told me Gregory had called her, but getting information from him was like pulling teeth. He was hoping I was at her house and going to visit on Thanksgiving Day, but I wasn't I was held up at a truck stop waiting for a snowstorm to pass.

Gregory was called out and told to go to the visiting room that the governor's people wanted to meet with him. He sat there for quite a long time and was told they were waiting for another member of the party who didn't show up so the meeting never happened. Gregory was pumped because of the attention to his case.

We had been in this same position before the previous governor died in a plane crash. Now it was nearing the end of the current governor's term and there was activity again on Gregory's case. After so many years of one disappointment after another, I must admit I wasn't as excited as Gregory probably was. Too many years had passed.

Though I believed that someday the Lord would deliver Gregory I really did not think this governor had the courage to do what was right. He would have to have the courage to expose the travesties for what they were in Gregory's case.

As a matter of fact, I was beginning to believe that one of the prerequisites for being a politician was cowardice because too many put their careers before doing what is right in the area of criminal justice. To allow a case like Gregory's to sit as it has with all the evidence proving corruption in the courts is more sinful than the crime he was charged with. Where are the true statesmen whose passion it is to serve and not to be served as the politicians of today who serve only their interests instead of the constituents in the community?

The Corrupt DEA Snitch

The following are the transcripts for a Frontline interview with Andrew Chambers. You can see in the following that Chambers was indeed working for the DEA He is noted for lying about himself and his criminal record when called to testify. He did not lie about Gregory's reaction to Ronald's shooting the people in the house, but that information was not allowed in at trial seeing the charge of 1st degree Criminal Assault of Andrew Chambers was nolle prose before the trial began. Therefore, Chambers' name should not have come

Chambers was an informant for the DEA for 16 years. He worked all over the country and is responsible for the arrest of 445 drug dealers and the seizure of 1.5 tons of cocaine, and $6 million in assets.

up, but the prosecution testified himself for Chambers to concoct the lie. Therefore it is so important for the accused to be able to confront their accusers. That is the only way jurors can get to the truth of the matter.

How does the exchange happen between the buyers and the suppliers?

You have a drug dealer who knows the Mexican, and the Mexican will bring the dope in. And when he brings it in, he might have 50 kilos. All 50 kilos might not be all that good. But 40 of them might be good. He'll split that 40 up, give 20 to one guy and 20 to another guy. They are his guys who pay on time. When they say it'll be two or three days, it'll be two or three days. So that money right there is almost accounted for. The other 10 might be dropped in some water, or maybe they're not that potent. So he would push that off to the guys who are not that dependable. But the dope was not that good, so he's not taking a real major loss on it. But the 40 that he's got is high-quality dope, and that has to be paid for. So now it gets to people in the inner city. Then the guys who got the first 20 starts supplying it to the middle guys, who are buying half a [kilo], maybe two [kilos]. That type of money is usually paid up front. So now you have this Mexican who's still waiting for his first 20 [kilos] to get back, because he has to get that money back to the main Mexicans across the border.

Do the dealers have a form of insurance?

Sometimes a Mexican might say, "Look here, give me your car. Give me something. You got the title to your car?" Because he don't want no car that ain't paid for. And he don't want no Mustang that's a 1970. You know, "Give me something new." It's just a big game, and it's how you're going to play the game, and who are the other persons you're dealing with. . . . The blacks know that the Mexicans have the dope, and the Mexicans know that they need to sell it to the blacks because they're the ones that are

109

*selling most of the dope in the United States. . . .
When you're dealing with anybody with this type of
dope, it's always some funny games going on. Because you know you might get two [kilos] from a guy
one day, and then next day, you get two more [kilos].
Well, the third day, you give him two [kilos], and then
he don't pay you back. So it's an operation that is not
all about being truthful, because it's a lot of games
being played. Nobody is saying, "Well, look here, I'm
going to let you hold on to my mother while I sell these
[kilos]." So it's no trust. It's just how you feel about a
guy and what you're trying to make.*

Is that where the violence comes in?

*Yeah, that's how a lot of Mexicans get killed,
because a black guy or somebody else might know
that this Mexican is sitting on 20 [kilos]. So when the
Mexican comes to talk to them, they'll snatch it, or kill
him, trying to find out where the dope is. That's why
you have a lot of gunplay.*

**Can you describe the payment system and the
clientele?**

*You can put dope in gas tanks. I've seen where
Mexicans have hooked up the whole front dashboard
of a car where you hit the button and the dashboard
comes down, and you have kilos laying all from one
end of the car to the other end of the car. They have
door panels where you got to put your foot on the
brake and put the car in neutral for the door handles
to pop open. These guys have talents, but their talents are for the wrong thing. But they have talents to
put kilos anywhere.*

**What was the situation like when you started
in St. Louis 15 or 16 years ago?**

110

Crack really was just getting started. It was still mostly powder. I think crack was really just getting ready to start around 1984, 1985. And for some reason, black people had a little bit more know-how about making money. I mean, the white people knew how to do it. But blacks knew how to make it work to a little bit more benefit. . . . Blacks had a little bit more finesse about making it work a little bit better. And then they switched it to crack, and it just went crazy. It was everywhere. It was crack city. You hear different people just talking about crack, crack this, crack that. Crack made everything else look like it wasn't nothing.

Has crack gone away?

No, it's not gone away. It's just that what happens, times start changing. And what happens is, with law enforcement, they start cracking down on crack. Crack gives a stiffer sentence than does powder. So now what happens is guys start learning that crack will get you more years than the powder will. So we better go back to the powder and just start selling powder now, but this crack will have you gone for a long time. It didn't burn itself out. The laws burned it out. So you got dope dealers saying, "I'm not going to do crack no more. I'm not going to sell crack, because crack is a higher sentence. But I'm going to keep on selling the powder."

How are the drugs dispersed from the time they enter the United States?

The Mexican who's across the border, his big boss says, look here, bring it on across to the United States. So he brings it across. And when he brings it across, he usually has another Mexican guy or whatever that's over here in the States. Now they'll bring it to a stash house or location or a warehouse that they got set up. They'll bring it in, and then they'll bring it to the guy who's going to host all this. And he's the one who's going to distribute all the dope out to everybody. When it gets to his place, he's making sure that everything is there. If it's supposed to be 1,000 or 2,000, he makes sure that all the dope is accounted for. Now the mule, his job is done. So he goes back. Now the host guy has the kilos.

The host is the guy who, when the Mexicans bring it over, he brings it over to a guy. And I call him the host, because he has control of all the dope, and he's the one who's making the phone call to different people telling them to come pick up they stash. Say the host has somebody in New Orleans. He'll call somebody and say, "Hey, my people just brought 2,000 keys from across the border. I have them here. Put in your order." Guy puts in his order. He says, "Okay, I want ten kilos." So he says, "Okay, ten kilos. For me to get them there to you is going to cost you $22,000. So $22,000, and then I'm sending somebody with them, so I'm putting on an extra $100 on every [kilo] that I send for my driver." The figure that I'm giving you is just figures; you know they can go high or low, it just depends on what the mule is taxing the guy for bringing them. What it's worth to him to bring them all the way down there, take that chance. So now, the people who the host distributes to come and they pick up their orders, 10 here, 20 here, 30 here, 40 here. And the host is telling them, "You got to have this back in 10 days, two weeks," or whatever.

He's got a little log. He's keeping everything down, who owes him, what owes him, and everything like that. The people who he distributes to are the guys who are selling in the inner city. So now he has a line of people that's buying what they call nine ounces—half a [kilo]—but all that money is coming up. That's no front money; that's being paid when it gets delivered. So it goes from that level to that level to that level, all the way until it hits the street, and then it's right back up the chain. . . .

How does dope travel from L.A. to the rest of the country?

The reason people come is because they know it's cheaper here in LA. You got people driving with their wives or their girlfriends, or saying they getting ready to go to Disneyland on vacation, and got a car full of kids. They're going to Disneyland, but the boyfriend or the girlfriend or whatever is going to go meet the supplier and get some dope, and then take it back to his home state with the kids in the car.

You might have a cousin or you might know somebody . . . I want to say that, to a point, dope dealers have like a little union. They all know each other in some type of way or some type of form. He might have some friends, and two of his friends got some relatives in Memphis. So the two guys here in L.A. say, "You know my buddy is coming down from Memphis, he's trying to get something." And the guy will say, "Okay, well, bring them to me." So the guy will come up from Memphis. It's all about word of mouth, who you know. It's not like you're just coming out here and you got a sign on your shoulder, saying, "Hey, I'm looking for a kilo. Can anybody help me?" It's not like that.

You have a Colombian guy and he's trying to find that connection. He's got 100 kilos that he don't mind saying, "Okay, look here. I'm going to give you one kilo to let you know that I'm for real." So the guy takes it. Nothing happens, because the drug dealers know that ain't no policeman going to give you no kilo. DEA, FBI, nobody, they're not going to give you a kilo and let you go sell it on the street. So if a dope dealer does that, then it's got to be legit.

If he fronts you one, then next time you might buy one. He might front you two more. And that's how you get started. That's how you build that relationship. Before you know it, you're buying five or ten kilos, paying for half of them, and getting fronted the rest. And the Mexican or the Colombian guy, oh, he loves it, because that means you come to see him every week. And every time you come to see him, you're bringing him $100,000, $50,000, whatever. And then you just build a great little relationship.

Isn't it dangerous to keep a couple of million dollars in cash in a house?

Yes, but you can't do nothing else with it. Can't take it to the bank. Usually, the people I dealt with, somehow they keep it in the ground. I knew one guy who built a safe and put it in the ground. All the money was in the ground in a big old safe.

In your experience, over the last 15 years, has it become easier or harder to get drugs on the street?

The difference is that people are a little bit more leery of you. It's easy to get it, but people ask more questions now than what they used to. They used not to ask no questions. . It's not harder to get. It's easy to get it.

114

Did you ever feel that maybe you've just helped keep the price of drugs up?

No, what I've been doing is to let people know that what they're doing is wrong, and you can get caught now. That's the issue. You can get caught. This is not free. A lot of times people think that you can do this and nothing is going to happen. You selling crack to kids, and mothers losing their houses, mothers losing their dignity and all this, and you think you won't get caught, but you will

But if drugs are still available everywhere, what good have you done?

You have to put some kind of effort out there to let people know that this is a dead end, that this is not right.

Does it help to lock them up?

Yes, because that's the only way they're going to learn. . . . If you got a problem with going to jail for 20 years, and you don't want to go to jail, then you shouldn't be selling this dope. You need to get you a job. Because this game here that you're playing will get you put in jail for the rest of your life. And then you're in jail, the first thing you think about, you be like, "Wow, I really didn't have to do that."

You are black. A disproportionate number of the people who go to jail for drug violations are black. How do you deal with that?

There's all kind of ways you can look at that. Because what happens is that you have a black guy selling dope. And the black guy, he's going to let you know that he's selling dope by him hanging in the streets, wearing all the fancy clothes, driving the cars, spending, $5000, $6,000 on rims for cars, a

115

$4,000 music system that you can hear four blocks away.

Now the white guy, he's a little bit more laid back. You know, he wants to go buy a car from the wreck yard, put it in his driveway, and then go to Home Depot somewhere and buy some tools and work on it. He's not going to be seen. He's going to try to put his money in to some type of savings or something like that. He's not going to go to his back-yard and dig a hole and put his money in there. That's where a lot of black guys get caught up, be-cause they advertise.

I hear that you grossed over $2 million. How did you get paid?

Right. It's just a percentage, of property, jew-elry, houses, cars, or whatever. If they were going to pay me pennies, I think I would have done the same thing. I might not have done it that long, but I believe I would have done the same thing. It's not a money issue, because I have kids. And I would hate for one of these guys to be selling crack to my daughter or my son.

But how much did you make over the 16 years?

They say two million. It could be less, it could be more, I'm not sure. I haven't really took the time out to give it an exact count.

The criticism of you is that you committed crimes you didn't admit to when you testified in cases.

That's what they said. They said that because I didn't say that I had been arrested for traffic tickets. I didn't know at that time that traffic tickets were an issue. . . . I was working when I got the solicitation. How can you be around a bunch of dope dealers and *police grab you and you say, "Hold on, I work for DEA." So you kind of got to take the tab a little bit, and just go with it. You can't burn your undercover role. That's what I'd been doing.*

I thought that it was better for me to take the little hitch on the solicitation than to say, "Hey, I work for DEA," and blow the cover. . . . A guy told me that if he knew that the money that I made, he would be doing it. You need more people out there like me to deal with these guys. Say the host knows he could have made $2 million. Don't you think he would have told the Colombian boy or the Mexican boy over there? He'd give him up quick. But he don't know that. You don't have billboards up saying, "We need informants." But if they knew what I did, it'd be a lot more dope dealers in jail; a lot more.

Because you were paid well?

Exactly

How much did you get paid?

How much I got paid? I think they said two million. I don't know. It's a funny situation, but that's what it takes. This is what you have to fight these people with. You can't fight these people with this being nice. FRONTLINE pbs online wgbh website copyright 1995-2006.

By

Gregory

After reading this interview I came away with more than one situation here. I can understand the DEA fight against drugs and wanting to eradicate this terrible cost of lives on a large scale. But, I am in the frame of thought with former Attorney General Janet Reno when she saw how corrupt this man was and she made it a point to suspend him indefinitely. This was the right thing for her to do. I know some would think that you have to crack a few eggs to scramble them. In their mind, they look at a situation that you must have some collateral damage. That is not their decision, because that is the reason we have rules of law and procedures.

I remember a situation one time where there was a big pothole on a road by a railroad track. Nowadays there are potholes everywhere. I saw the city workers filling in potholes and I asked if they were going to fill in the one by the railroad track, and they said, "No." The reason they wouldn't do it was because they felt it was the railroad's responsibility. When I realized they were not going to do anything, I decided to fill it myself to protect the cars that were coming through. I didn't have the equipment to do it, so I used dirt and gravel and filled it in the best I could. A railroad officer came by and noticed me doing this. He asked me what I was doing. I explained to him that the city wouldn't fill in this hole, so I was doing it to keep cars from being damaged. He was so impressed that someone would take the time to be concerned about others that he said, "I'll get it done!" Two weeks or so later the hole was filled in.

Andrew Chambers was a 'flim flam' man even though he was well-meaning in helping his brother's memory by helping to put away drug dealers and ridding the cities of dangerous drugs. It appears he was helping himself to a large sum of money. The real problem though is all the innocent lives that the Feds and State would like to pass off as collateral damage. I understand that Chambers sometimes entrapped people that weren't even drug dealers into his world and even the government didn't always take time to sift through it. That is why I am impressed with what Janet Reno did in the case of Andrew Chambers.

If people commit crimes they should be expected to do the time and no normal thinking person should have a problem with that. When you have this type of activity going on in our judicial process then you have overzealous prosecutors like George Peach and Garrett Randall and judges like Robert Dierker who skirt the rules to put innocent people in prison. This they do while cooperating with the DEA. Breaking all procedural rules of law, discovery, due process, and rules of ethics knowing they have absolute immunity. This should not be the case.

When President Reagan started the war against drugs, mistakes were going to be made understandably. In this situation, Janet Reno was correct because the use of a documented liar in the courtroom taints the process. Chambers' lies nearly always revolved around himself and who he was.

In the Oliver case once it became aware to the state who Chambers was they had an ongoing responsibility to disclose this information to the defense. The moment they chose not to that trial could not proceed any further...untainted. Concocting a story was not the solution.

CHAPTER 13
Jailhouse Penal Solutions
by
Gregory

As we know it the penal system began in the United States in 1891 with the "Three Prisons Act" which created the Federal Prison System. The first three prisons were in Leavenworth, McNeil Island, and Atlanta. These prisons were under the supervision of the Department of Justice. The individual states, however, established their prison before that with the first one being Walnut Street Prison in Philadelphia, Pennsylvania, which was established in 1773. The first prison in the state of Missouri was the Missouri State Penitentiary, built in 1836. This was my first prison dwelling after I was wrongfully convicted. It was the first Prison built west of the Mississippi River and was known as the bloodiest 47 acres west of the Mississippi.

Because this was my first prison dwelling, I had a lot of adjusting to do. Not only did I have to deal with the conditions of being housed with many violent offenders and witnessing fights daily, but we had to deal with the physical environment filled with roaches, rodents, musty air, asbestos walls, peeling paint. Inferior HVAC causing it to be hot in the summer and freezing in the winter. There were many broken windows that let in the heat and cold from outside.

The food mainly was prepared by other inmates and supervised by underpaid outside staff causing it to be an unhealthy environment. People who should not have been handling food were handling it. The dining room was overcrowded and was a death trap where many fights and sometimes riots would break out.

Some inmate's pastime was spent creating programs trying to help rehabilitate other inmates. These programs were sometimes adopted by the administration to show their superiors that they were trying to do things to rehabilitate the prison population. I have always believed as I matured in Christ that **education without regeneration is devastation.** This became more apparent to me as men who went through the inmate-created programs returned to prison. The men who were released found themselves right back in the system. Why? Because there was no room for regeneration of the soul in programming God's people. The programming of God's people only incurs a temporary change and lasts until the person comes to a place of frustration again and falls into the same traps that got them there in the first place.

One of these programs brought in victims and victim's families. It had the inmates apologize for acts that another inmate had done to these victims and their families. This bothered me because it was not true contrition of wrongdoing for the acts that they themselves had committed. No matter how sincere they might have sounded and the many tears that echoed pain for the victims and their families—there was never any closure for either party. Many of the inmates participated in these types of programs to make the administration believe that they were changed men when actually they were just conditioned men for a season. The season lasted until after they were released from prison. Conditioning a heart is not changing a heart and a changed heart is what is needed for a person to be converted to a more righteous path.

I spent six years in the military and understood the military discipline and respect it had for authority. What bothered me about one of the programs is that they would have men marching to cadence as soldiers would as though this would bring discipline to the inmate's lives. Many of the inmate leaders who were over the men were not always respectful of authority themselves, nor of right activity. It was just a routine that made the inmates feel that by marching to a rhythm that they were accomplishing something. Their goal—by doing all these things it would break their criminal behavior from their thinking. What they did not realize is that most of the criminal behavior had become a learned choice, which left out individual accountability. The question is who were they accountable to?

This was not the only program. There was a mixture of several programs and as an inmate completed a program, he punched a ticket and it looked good on his record, but how many write-ups did they get in the meantime. I did not participate in any of these programs because in my heart I knew they were not right. One of the things that stood out to the governor when they investigated my case was that in over 20 years, I had only gotten three *minor* write-ups. Some of the inmates that participated in these programs, had many major write-ups throughout their prison stay. On the surface, whether in prison or on the street, people can make themselves look like a good person, but the Lord looks at your heart because your heart will eventually shape your behavior.

The correctional officers (CO's) for the most part did their jobs and many of them were respected by the inmates. Some CO's were so in tune with the men and what was needed to be done they knew the inmates that were trouble and the ones that were not. If you wanted a good evaluation of a particular inmate check with the CO's, not their paperwork alone. What is needed to really help these inmates is not to be conformed to a program, but to be transformed by the renewal of the mind in the Word of God, which will be the catalyst to a changed life.

During the Reagan Administration, the "War Against Drug Policy" began. On the surface, it looked to be well-meaning, but along with that he also started the private prisons to warehouse the influx of drug offenders and their so-called conspirators. He was also instrumental in shutting down many of the mental institutions, which created another problem causing the mentally ill to be dumped into the prison system. If not there then they were left to the streets, which caused a different set of problems to society. Just like any institution, there can be improvements or changes, but to do away with things and not replace them with a better solution is a disaster waiting to happen.

One day when I was praying and wondering why I was in this situation among so many different negative characters and personalities, the Lord showed me that the prison was like a *small* fishbowl and I was a fish in this bowl swimming amongst sharks and they could not harm me. The good news was that He was going to release me from this *small* bowl and, bring me out into the *larger* bowl (of society) where I would know how to deal effectively with the many sharks in the world. Bonnie did not know what the Lord showed me, and as she advocated for me to the governor, she used a fishbowl. She handed the governor's chief counsel a fishbowl full of requests to let me out and told the chief council that, "Gregory is one fish worth pulling out of the muck and mire." The governor's chief counsel told me when he met with me at the prison that I had some good advocates.

I like to get to the root of a subject rather than the fruit of a thing, and when we talk about the penitentiary, the root word for penitentiary is "penance". Which means repentance. The system was designed to be an instrument to help men and women come to a place of repentance before restoring them back to society. When the for-profit prisons began, it shifted away from the original intent of repentance or reforming and turned its focus to the all mighty dollar and it became a place of warehousing people for profit. These prisons are now on the stock market and many a politician has built their careers on being 'tough on crime.' Even in MSP, you could see early on that they were moving towards this as they built factories and industries within the prisons to use the prisoners as cheap labor. The communities started seeing how profitable this was and began to sell this idea. As profit became the focus, human value diminished.

Although slavery had been abolished, men found a loophole through the Thirteenth Amendment to enslave those that were incarcerated, both black and white. It seemed to be disproportionate though based not only on prison statistics but on sentences rendered. The Black man/woman got longer sentences than the Hispanic man/woman and the Hispanic man/woman got a heavier sentence than a White man/woman for the same crime in many cases.

13th Amendment

Section 1. Neither slavery nor involuntary servitude, except as a punishment for crime whereof the party shall have been duly convicted, shall exist within the United States, or any place subject to their jurisdiction.

Section 2. Congress shall have power to enforce this article by appropriate legislation.

"Therefore, when an innocent person is placed in our prison system, (such as myself and others), they have totally violated the 13th Amendment. It gives congress or any governing body the jurisdiction to enforce the proper remedies for holding those accountable who violate this amendment and/or the rights of citizens in the states thereof. The reason this is stated is because if we are a Nation that is to be governed by laws—these laws shall not be abridged at the whim of men/women who choose to profiteer through the suffering of other people." Gregory Oliver May 2021

Based upon the 13th Amendment our constitution leaves no mistake that the system is not systemically racist. Our system has been manipulated by men and women through tricks and traps to cause people to misuse it for gain, be it power or monetary gain. The reason our framers were specific in their intent was to make sure that these types of things would not be the case—causing chaos in our society. To quote the title of one of Dr. Martin Luther King Jr's. book "Where Do We Go from Here; Chaos or Community?"

✝

"Injustice anywhere is a threat to justice everywhere." Dr. Martin Luther King Jr.

"It is not possible to be in favor of justice for some people and not be in favor of justice for all people." Dr. Martin Luther King Jr.

The United States has one of the largest prison systems in the world. There are over two million people incarcerated throughout the prison population. This has been a real problem economically and in other ways and has affected our society. It has affected the lives of people who live in the United States. Many think it is racially motivated, but I believe that it is economically motivated more than just racially motivated. I believe, it takes someone to really take the time to dissect the situation to try and figure it out. For years, they have always known that the population problem in our prison system has been a real thorn. Even now the Prison System is on the stock market that is why we have private prisons, many try to keep it on the low, low. It is really a problem when you see how people have changed the prison system. It has gone from the penal system to an economic system. The penal system was designed to allow people to be incarcerated for crimes and wrongs they have done in hopes that over time the punishment will cause a person to reform, and the system will balance itself out. But that is not what it is anymore. I think we need to look at it. If we are going to be "*Walking Free*," we need to deal with that and we also need to deal with the subject of racism. Racism today as they are trying to portray it is not the racism of the 1960s. You have politicians using this for political means, and that is a problem because it is a power struggle and when power is mixed in with it you have a system of deception that is in the center of it.

The civil rights movement of the 60's did a great deal for beginning the healing process. Although this work was not completed. Dr. Martin Luther King Jr. saw the need of reconciling the differences between white and black. Unfortunately, he was murdered before this reconciliation took place. We as Christians have the ministry of reconciliation and we need to be that example for our communities. When

127

we do this the racial divide will diminish in hopes that in the future it will be eradicated. A godly love will cover a multitude of sins and hatred that neighbors have one towards another. This is the method in which we can leave a legacy for our young people who struggle daily with who they are and how they are to treat their peers. We do not have to teach critical race theory in any schools, organizations, or anywhere for that matter. That was not part of the true civil rights movement of the 60's and should not be part of it in the 21st century. Racism is wrong. Hatred is wrong and if we force it on our neighbors it is a form of bullying. Any God fearing person knows that God would have us love one another in spite of the color of one's skin, gender or ethnic background.

CHAPTER 14

Prison Codes

by

Gregory

1. Do not interfere with an inmate's interest. Never rat on an inmate, do not be nosy, do not have loose lips, and never put an inmate on the spot.

2. Do not fight with other inmates. Do not lose your head; do your own time.

3. Do not exploit inmates. If you make a promise, keep it, do not steal from inmates, do not sell favors, and do not go back on bets.

4. Maintain yourself. Do not: weaken, whine, cop-out. Be a man and be tough.

5. Do not trust guards or the things they stand for. Do not be a sucker, the officials are wrong, and the prisoners are right.

6. Do not interact with the guards, because you might be considered a snitch.

The preceding is a list of basic codes, but more develop sometime unknown until you overstepped the line. As I went through the prison system, the Lord gave me favor...those codes didn't seem to apply to me. Basic respect was my code throughout my incarceration. For instance: I had started a Bible study and prayer group on the yard and men began to see the Lord answer prayers and wanted to join, but along with the inmates that wanted the Lord in their life there were men who wanted to disrupt the prayer group to try and lure young men away for sexual favors. We called these inmates 'booty bandits' and I let them know that they were not going to lure these guys away as long as they were in this prayer group. That was considered violating 'interfering with an inmate interest.' Although, to come up on my prayer group was also 'interfering with an inmate interest.'

I was working in the kitchen one night and an inmate that use to sing in the choir with me came up and said, "Big O, I need to talk to you."

"What is it?"

"I need your help."

"Okay, what can I do for you?'

"I got involved with the homosexual lifestyle and thought I would like it, but then this guy started selling me to other men."

"What!" I said. I was outraged. So, I asked the Lord, *"Lord I need to do something, what can I do."* And the Lord said in an audible voice to me.

"Pray about it." So I did just that I prayed for him. The next day this guy ran up to me and said, "I don't know what you did, but guess what? The guy that was selling me off to other guys. Said that his parents who were Christians called up to the prison and asked for him to call home, so he did, and they told him.

"Whatever it is that you are doing up there, STOP IT NOW!" He tried to deny it, but they knew, and they told him again "NO, you need to STOP it NOW!" They did not even go into details with him, they just knew. He told the Christian brother that "you don't have to be a homosexual anymore; you can go free. Oh—but before you go, will you pray with me so I can get to know this Jesus that you know?" Again, by the favor of God, I was able to 'interfere with an inmate's interests,' which was proof that I didn't have to follow the prison codes.

✠

I didn't go out of my way to break the codes, but if evil was being done and the Lord wanted me to deal with it, I followed His directive. That brings me to this last story. There was a time when I had gotten to the honor dorm which was in four house, and my Cellie and I were watching TV. We heard some commotion in the common area. Across the way, from us, an inmate was stabbing another inmate with an ice pick. The Lord told me to go and stop him.

"What, Lord?"

"Go and stop him!"

So, I put my shoes on and started heading that way to stop him. My cellmate and few others looked and shouted at me saying, "What are you doing?"

"The Lord told me to go stop him!"

"Are you crazy?" They said. I just kept walking to do what the Lord told me to do. As soon as I got close to him someone mentioned the man's name who was wielding the ice pick and I shouted.

"Jerry!" He turned around and looked at me in terror and ran with the ice pick dripping with blood. I turned around and went back to my cell. All the inmates who witnessed this got so mad at me they didn't talk to me for two weeks. They told me he could have turned on you man and hurt you and then they would have had to get involved to protect me.

I told them, "The Lord didn't tell you to do it, He told me to stop that man."

CHAPTER 15
Bullying
by
Gregory

Bullying according to Webster's Dictionary is;: *abuse and mistreatment of someone vulnerable by someone stronger, more powerful, etc.: the actions and behavior of a bully"* We look at a world today filled with bullies that are all ages and from all walks of life. As we look at Webster's Dictionary's definition of the bully, we see this bullying playing out throughout our society today. Have you ever heard the media say, "that the president should use the "bully pulpit" to deal with a particular issue? It is because our culture has become so readily accepting of the bully mentality in a variety of venues, that it has become accepted in society. The Scripture says,

> *"**Righteousness** exalteth a **nation**: but sin is a reproach to any people." "The LORD is far from the wicked: but he heareth the prayer of the **righteous**." ... "But in every **nation** he that feareth him, and worketh **righteousness**, is accepted with him."* (Proverbs 14:34)

As a matter of fact, just recently, President Biden was talking about taking President Trump behind the shed. This is a bullying tactic. Now do not get me wrong, I do not want to politicize this I just want to bring out a factor that BULLYING IS WRONG! Many people probably laughed at what he said because they don't see him as the tough guy even though he is the president. A president needs to lead a nation—not bully the nation.

Many of us probably remember in school when we had to, or we knew someone who had to deal with a bully. Even Mike Tyson at one time had a bully pick on him when he was younger. That caused him to learn how to fight. Unfortunately, his fighting style is bullish, but it shaped and molded him in ways that later affected him negatively.

I had to deal with my own bullies when one day they decided to take their bullying from the schoolyard right to my back door. That was a mistake! It was at that point that the bullies (2 of them) realized that their bullying days were over. I took on both and sent them packing. I had no more problems with bullying again—that is until the state of Missouri decided to bully me.

I did an interview with a woman's group that was concerned about all types of bullying and especially the rise in cyberbullying. They took their message to the street in Grand Rapids, Michigan. It was successful. The leader of the group had me speak on the podcast news show so that we could get the word out. In that interview, I pointed out how we have allowed bullies to slip through the cracks. No longer are bullies just in the schoolyard, they are in our government, on our jobs, in our neighborhoods, even in our churches, there are even some executives in some companies who style of leadership is bullyish, and there is cyberbullying. Then there are some that have put on a uniform and are on our police force or they are in the judiciary either prosecuting a case or sitting on the judge's bench and we have given them the bully pulpit just like the news media encourages our president to use the bully pulpit at times. I am not saying that we need to let the bully rule your life. What I am saying is that you must stand up for yourself during these times when faced with a bully.

I did some boxing in my day while growing up in the inner city of St. Louis. I learned how to handle myself and sometimes I had to fight more than one person at a time. When I was wrongfully incarcerated, I ran into a different type of bully who could break laws and violate constitutional rights, and all I could think of was that I needed to fight this bully off. After years of struggling in this different arena with how I was to fight this new type of bully, the Lord asked me, "When are you going to let Me fight your battles?"

I told one Christian brother what the Lord told me. He said, "What's wrong with you...you can't do that in a prison setting?" Because one of the codes in prison is...you must be tough if you are going to survive. I didn't argue with him.

I just went about my business and the Lord spoke to me again and said, "if you can't trust me in prison, you won't be able to trust me outside of prison." I learned when the Lord tells me something He is *always* right. There was nothing left for me to do but to trust the Lord. Thank God that I did, because then the Lord taught me a valuable lesson about meekness. He let me know that meekness was not weakness, but it was strength under control. The Scripture says,

> "*He that is slow to anger is better than the mighty; and he that ruleth his spirit than he that taketh a city.*" (Proverbs 16:32)

Wouldn't it be nice if the rioters and all the misguided angry people we have in the country today understood this principle because it would give them the right perspective on how to control their anger and get the right result rather than burning down their cities and costing the taxpayers exponentially.

I had to deal with bullies when I was in city jail. One was a top mob boss, and I didn't back down—I stood up for myself and the other men that were being bullied by him. I had a couple of bullying situations happen while I was at city jail. I also stood up against two inmates who were taking other inmates' phone time when they were trying to make a call. I told them, "When I come out to use the phone, I don't want to hear a word." I still don't back down to bullies, because in most cases they are covering up insecurity or weakness by trying to be tough. By standing up to him it exposes those weaknesses so healing can take place.

Our parents bought us bikes when we were young. One of our bikes got stolen while it was sitting outside the store we went to. We saw a boy riding on our bike, and we told him, "Hey, you'd better give us our bike back!" This boy who had our bike was a member of a small gang called the Aldine Gang. That did not scare us, he still had to turn over the bike. So, the boy came to the front of our house with friends from the gang, about six or seven of them. "We're gonna fight for it and whoever wins gets the bike," one of the gang bullies said.

My dad said, "Tell them to meet you all around in the back." There were two of my brothers and myself and they numbered six or seven. That didn't bother us because we were on *our turf*. The fight was on and we were all over the place whipping these guys. We used whatever we could get our hands on to fight, I think I grabbed a rake. The whole time my dad just sat there under the tree, not getting excited...just watching...he let us take care of business. When it was over the bike was still in our back yard and the group of boys had run off. My dad said to me, "Boy, the next time find you a short stick, something you can handle."

I asked my dad, "Why did you just sit there?"

He lifted his shirt and showed me the pistol he had up under it. In other words, everything was under control. I learned two valuable lessons that day. Even when we think things have gotten out of control or it is not what we think it should be.

My first lesson; my dad showed me he had things under control, just like the Lord has things under control even when we do not.

My second lesson; was that you must stand up to bullies—once you do, they will respect you. We never had any more problems with the Aldine Gang and word got around "Don't mess with the Oliver brothers."

Today we have bullies in everything. People might not understand this, but big tech is trying to bully Americans out of their 1st Amendment rights. They can call it whatever they want, but anytime the seemingly powerful abuse and mistreat the established rights of others—even if they think they are going after a bully—their tactics become bullyish.

When the state of Missouri allowed a corrupt prosecutor, George Peach, to abuse his authority simply because he was angry at something my granddad did. It was clear that my brother had mental issues and that I was an innocent man, but Mr. Peach vowed that we would never see the light of day because my granddad tried to get his attention when he called him on the phone and tried to pass himself as Senator "Jett" Banks as he pleaded for justice for Ronald and I. It was wrong for my granddad to do that, but in his mind, he was just trying to take care of his family. The law is still the law, and we entrust it to the hands of officials, believing that they will conduct themselves with integrity...regardless of their feelings. They must honor the 'rule of law.' Mr. Peach did not do this in my brothers and my case. In our case, he used his office as a bully pulpit in the courts. He forced the officers under him to concoct stories no matter the cost to ensure a conviction that otherwise would not have happened. Sometimes there is a lot of pressure from the victim's family put on the state to get a conviction. In my case the family was given a false narrative to run with for someone...anyone to be punished regardless of whether it is the right somebody or not.

Mr. Peach was doing this while operating in illicit behavior. His second in command, Garrett Randall, our trial prosecutor handled the credit card that Mr. Peach used for illicit sex and misappropriation of government funds. We know this because; during the deposition of Garrett Randall, he let this information come out to my attorneys while being deposed—for the record. I can understand that Mr. Randall might not have wanted to confront his boss by telling him that he couldn't take a case personally and send a man away for the rest of his life simply because he was upset. Not only that, but it cost my brother his life. This bullying tactic I cannot let this slide by.

When we received the governor's file in 2019 from the AAG we found out that the victim's family was notified that they were thinking of releasing me and they wanted feedback from the family of the deceased. The family of the deceased was split and some of the reasons for being against my freedom was because they received a false narrative about my case from the beginning. Their letters read like the testimony of the ringer hearsay on hearsay witness, Ernest Fields who was related to the deceased and one probably two of the jurors. The AAG Gregory Goodwin in the 19th Circuit Court did not want us to have this file. He was given it because he was looking for something that would show me in a negative light because the deposition of Garrett Randall didn't go well for the state. This file proved my innocence to the point that he asked my lawyers to destroy it...trying to claim it was a work product. This is a form of bullying on the highest level of judicial misconduct.

I understand why people got upset with what happened with George Floyd and Breanna Taylor and others, and how advocates get behind certain cases, but mine is a case that has been going on for over thirty years. We went through every state remedy giving them the chance for even one person to honestly look at the merits of my case and no one would until the governor's office did. Because they proved I was innocent, they should have pardoned me but instead, I was given a lesser charge making me eligible for parole.

Never in all my efforts to clear my name did I ever use the 'race card,' which in itself is a form of bullying and laying on guilt trips. I didn't need to...I had too much information against the state. What boggles my mind is Judge Daniel Green of the 19th Circuit County Court in Jefferson City, Missouri, had my case in the court for over 5 years and even helped secure some of the damning evidence against the state, but refused to consider the merits of my case. It was as though he was saying that because the case was over 30 years old that it didn't warrant the proper redress due to not wanting to air out other people's dirty laundry and abuse of the system.

A good leader when realizing an error within the system will correct it without needing to be told to, because it is the right thing to do, especially when dealing with people's lives. When he/she does right the wrong then trust is built within the system and the community in ways that will create a healing factor. This healing factor goes far beyond the problems our society is facing today. It would be hard for people to claim systemic racism if one or two bullies are dealt with at the onset. When others protect them for whatever reason a false narrative is created as we see playing out today.

The events of today boggles the minds of common-sense thinking people regardless of their race, gender, or creed, because as a believer we know that all have sinned, but when we generalize and say all are racist, or all are white supremacist it is not even close to reality. The Bible says a little leaven, leavens the whole lump. This means a little wickedness, just like yeast mixes in and works itself into the whole and affects all. Again, the Word says, *"righteousness exalts a nation, but sin* (wickedness) *is a reproach to all people."* Therefore, it is understandable why people were so offended when they saw a video of an officer with his knee on a man's neck regardless of his skin color.

My brother was said to have been strangled by two guards because it was hidden away in a prison and there has been no determination of the real cause of death. He was shipped off to the hospital to hide the place of death. Let the court of public opinion decide what really happened. We can determine the discrepancy from his death certificate. I can understand that the state would want to sweep all of this under the rug, but they have had over 30 years to correct the wrong, rectify the situation in the right way, but have chosen not to, because of wanting to hold an erroneous verdict intact.

"Man must evolve for all human conflict a method which rejects revenge, aggression, and retaliation. The foundation of such a method is love." Dr. Martin Luther King Jr.

CHAPTER 16
Channel 25/ Over the Road
by
Bonnie

The years had worn heavy and only faith and belief that the Lord would bring about the victory was the only thing that kept me going. I had bounced from job to job, mostly minimum wage jobs which was not enough money to keep a household going. I was working as a cashier at a supermarket and one day a customer came through the line she was excited about her new job. I started making conversation with her about it and found out where she was working because they were hiring at a higher rate than I was making. A couple of days later I went down to the factory and applied for a job. The human resource head interviewed me and looked at my education and asked, "Bonnie why are you applying for a job here?"

"I am over-educated, under qualified, fifty years old and I am not too proud to ask." I was hired on the spot...to start the following week. Factory work was a challenge for sure. I stood on my feet 10 hours a day in the same spot inspecting brass plated parts for faucets and chrome parts for cars. While I was working at the factory, I was offered a job at the Christian television station in New Bloomfield, MO. It wasn't making as much as I was making at the factory, but I would have a chance to minister and would be eight miles from the prison that Gregory was in. Lester the owner of the TV station helped families of inmates. They were in the middle of a large campaign for a young woman who killed a man who had been terrorizing her and killed her dogs.

I joined the ministry during the campaign to try and get the governor to release her. Lester gave out our 800 number to anyone who was interested in the case. He had information folders made up to hand out to anyone who called into the station. The phones didn't stop all day. I could barely get a breather. I was frustrated because Gregory hadn't shot anyone. While I was answering the hundreds of phone calls, the Lord spoke very clearly and impressed upon me that I was sowing seeds for Gregory's freedom. So, for the remainder of the calls for the rest of the day, I was just as pleasant as can be.

While I was in New Bloomfield, I was able to talk to Gregory every night and visit him every weekend. One day I walked to work because my tags had expired on my car and I was waiting for them to come in the mail. I was only in Missouri temporarily, so my car was registered in Michigan. I had to pass a wooded area along the way. A beautiful blond dog came out of the woods and up to me. I was a little nervous about a strange dog, but then I realized she was okay. She followed me all the way to the TV station and stayed outside. When Lester came into work, he asked about the dog. I told him she followed me to work. He then told me to find her some food and kept coaxing me to take her home with me. He kept saying, "Bonnie I know strays and that is a good one. You need to take her home." My car tags came in the mail, so I walked home to get my car, Then I drove back to the station and picked up the dog. I figured if I were going to have a dog, I would take her up to the dollar store and get her a dollar collar, dollar leash, dollar dog dish, and some dog food. Then I went back to the station and the beautiful blond dog I realized was actually a Brittany Spaniel but a very unusual one. She looked like a miniature golden retriever. She had a black nose and was black around the eyes which were really unusual because Brittany's usually had liver color nose and eyes and were spotted. She hung around the station the rest of the afternoon. When the workday was over, I loaded up Brittany [I thought that was a good name for a Brittany.] and told her I was taking her to the Taco Bell and if she passed the Taco Bell test I would take her home with me. Brittany and I sat on the grass and ate dinner at the Taco Bell. I decided if she liked Taco Bell then I would keep her. Of course, she passed the test.

That night when Gregory called, I was able to tell him about the dog. Right away he asked me to put the phone up to her ear so he could talk to her and get her use to hearing his voice. I put the phone to her ear, and she just looked at the phone. You could tell she was listening to him. It came time for us to say our prayers and I had a large pillow at the foot of my bed that I called my prayer pillow. I knelt down then suddenly Brittany sat down next to me and put her paws on the bed one paw over the other then she put her head on her paws as though she was saying her prayers too. It was as though she was praying, "Oh, Lord thank you for my new people friend." As near as I could figure from her teeth and everything else about her, she was about 11 months old.

✝

The Lord let me know I had to go back to Michigan and go see my parents I was to help them while my father was dying. I rented a U-Haul and loaded it up. As I always do, I slipped out in the middle of the night. I took Brittany with me, my parents loved dogs as much as I did so I was not worried about them accepting her. My father was failing. He had a couple of heart attacks already and was doing poorly. When we arrived, Brittany made a big hit and she and my dad hit it off.

For the next five years, I lived with my parents. During this time, I helped my parents with everything. My father was not able to take care of the house like he used to do.

I was able to secure the best-paying job I had since I graduated from Wheaton. My new job was working as a temporary employee at Michigan State University it was a little above minimum wage. In that job, I moved from department to department filling in where I was needed. I also worked a part-time job at a Christian Book Store during the week. By this time, I was 55 years old. Retirement wasn't even on the horizon, especially with the huge student loan payments.

My father passed away about eight months after I moved back home. On weekends, I had to take care of cutting the grass and trimming shrubs and trees on the three acres of property my father and mother developed. They were still living in the home my father built for my mother. The property was a lot of work, and I was on my own taking care of it. In the spring and fall, my sister's family would come out for a mass clean-up on the property getting it ready for spring and winter. In the winter, I did all the snow plowing too with my dad's John Deere. The hardest part was removing the lawn mower deck and putting on the plow blade and the chains on for winter, but I made it through. What time I had left on the weekends I took my mother wherever she wanted to go. I lived cooped up in my bedroom without even my own closet. There was no room for anything, my mother was a pack rat and after my father died, she started pulling out all of her treasures and had them stacked everywhere, and there was no place for anyone to sit. That meant there was never any company. I didn't build too many friendships because I was too embarrassed to invite anyone over. What does a person do when they are over-educated, underqualified, and in their mid-fifties? I applied for a job in Grand Rapids where my sister lived. She worked at Calvin College, so I applied for a job there and got it. My sister was nearing retirement age and would be able to help me with my mother when she retired. I got the job and started commuting from Williamston, Michigan to Grand Rapids every day for work in the wintertime. I now had a real job and made more than my job at Michigan State and my part-time job combined.

One weekend I was so burned out, I went off on my mother and I told her I was going to take her to Grand Rapids and set her up with a work friend's husband who was a realtor. I told her she had to get a place in Grand Rapids seeing that is where both my sister, Barb, and I worked. That next Monday I took my mother to work and had her connect with my friend's husband...it worked! My mother found a large condominium that would hold her treasures. Once the purchase of the condo was completed, I moved to the lower level with a roll-a-way bed to sleep on. I lived there during the week and on the weekends, I drove to Williamston to take care of the property and take my mother on her weekend excursions. We scheduled an auction to get rid of some of my mother's treasures in the barn and the house which took time. I lived alone in the condo about a year before my mother moved in. I was on a trip down to visit Gregory when they held the auction...only she didn't get rid of very much. It took many trips to get my mother moved in, but before she moved in, I had lost my job. I was without work again, but I kept looking. By this time, I was 58 years old. Now it was what do you do at 58 when you are over-educated and under-qualified?

My sister had recommended truck driving. She knew how much I liked driving and that I had a bit of a vagabond spirit. I mentioned the idea to my son; Bill and he, too, thought it would be a good idea. I went to the unemployment office because I had heard that they help with truck driver training. She asked me more than once if I really understood what I was getting into.

"Yes, I do," I responded.

She pursued further making sure I really knew what I was getting into because the Unemployment Office trained many people, but they never lasted once they realize what a hard, lonely life and over-the-road (OTR) truck driver's life is like.

The training proved to be challenging indeed. I had to take the general written test for my class A CDL driver's license, then I had to pass tests for my knowledge of air brakes, and hazmat in order to get my permit. I could do everything else, but backing was a challenge for me. I passed my test though and I was now officially a truck driver.

My first training job was with Covenant Transport, headquartered in Chattanooga, Tennessee. I went through their training and was assigned a mentor. Amanda was her name. She was a big woman and I liked her instantly. She had her dog riding with her, which was great. I wanted to have my dog running with me too. Amanda really knew the ropes and taught me an awful lot. I ran with her for 6 weeks. We ran from Los Angeles to Brooklyn, New York. One time we even got to the Mexican border with enough time to do some shopping in Mexico. I discovered the peculiarities of running in the different states. In New Jersey I learned you had to stay right to turn left. That was the most valuable lesson when driving a big rig. We ran North and South, through all sorts of weather. The worst snowstorm we hit I was driving, we were in Kansas City, Missouri during rush hour. Good training...I made it without incident.

When I finished training, they wanted me to run as a team with a stranger... I refused to do that. Seeing I was already experienced with my CDL, I called Swift Transportation in the Kansas City, Missouri area. They told me they would set me up with a mentor for three weeks then give me my own truck. That is exactly what happened, and I could take my dog, Brittany with me. This was in 2003. My first truck was a Freightliner, Columbia. I loved it! Believe it or not, I fixed it up real girly like.

Communication with Greg would be different during this season. He had to call collect and that was not a function on cell phones then. We worked out a system where Greg would call my friend Fae and tell her what he needed her to tell me. Then she in turn would call and update me. The system was not perfect by any means, but it was all we had under the circumstances.

CHAPTER 17
The Decision
by
Gregory & Bonnie

After my visit with Greg, I was concerned because I was going to go to Prague for the holidays to see my new granddaughter. I would be gone if anything had happened with Gregory's case. I prayed and believed that the Lord would hold everyone off until after I got back on the 29th of December. I was antsy about the trip and was wondering what was going to happen with Gregory's case. I prayed that they wouldn't do what they did with the last end of term with the preceding governor when they just sent Gregory's case over to the next administration after not making a decision.

By
Gregory

When Bonnie visited me after her trip to Prague I was excited to tell her what had transpired. I told her "This is the second time a governor's Chief Counsel came to meet with me.

"Really?"

"Yes, and what was interesting is that the Lord went before me. Gov. Holden's Chief Counsel asked me questions about my case and near the end of the meeting he told me, 'The governor wants to commute your sentence.' I quickly told him I am innocent. He said, 'I know, but this is what the governor wants to do. My heart sunk in my chest because I knew that I couldn't make the governor change his mind. It would have to be his team or God to change his mind. I didn't want to seem argumentative, and I was concerned that I might have pushed the issue at the meeting a bit. I continued to be kind and thankful and it wasn't until the Chief Counsel left that I wanted to let you know that you needed to let the governor's people know I appreciated them."

Sometime later while Bonnie and I were visiting, one of the correctional officers who had been following my case, and who knew that the governor commuted my sentence asked me if he could write a letter to the board on my behalf. I told him, "Yes I would appreciate it that you would do something like that for me."

Two days before the governor left office, I was eating in the prison dining room with other inmates. I was near the window, and I looked up in the sky and five geese flew overhead. I immediately told the men, "Those five geese mean something, but I don't know what." I remembered years ago a little girl named, Christy Beth told Bonnie that she saw me being released from prison and it had something to do with five. Bonnie was attending Northern Illinois University at the time while she was staying with Christy Beth and her mom. I kept that in my heart so when I saw the five geese, I was reminded of it. Two days later Governor Bob Holden commuted five inmate sentences. I was one of those five inmates.

On January 6, 2005, the governor of Missouri signed my clemency papers commuting my sentence from life without parole (the walking death penalty) to life with parole making me eligible immediately for parole. We were thrilled, but I knew I had to continue to fight once I was on the street. The commutation only acted as relaxing the sentence on someone who was getting the commutation for good behavior. That wasn't the case...yes...I had a near-perfect record, but the fact is that I was innocent, and they fabricated evidence against me to get two wins for the price of one. The governor should have given me a Full Pardon. Yet I am thankful because I know I get to fight another day.

by

Bonnie

I was driving for Swift Transportation at the time. I was sitting at our Manteno, Illinois terminal to get a trailer tire fixed. While I was waiting on the mechanics to finish the job, I received a phone call.

"Hello."

"Is this Bonnie?"

"Yes, it is."

"This is Mr. Mitchell. Do you remember me?"

Of course, I did. He was head of Probation and Parole in Missouri, who I worked so well with. Shortly after taking Gregory's case to the governor, President Bush appointed him to be one of the head people in the Federal Probation and Parole Office in Washington D.C. His promotion and move to Washington, though great for him, was a crushing blow to us and our cause.

"Yes sir, of course, I do."

"Well, I am calling to congratulate you for Gregory's commutation." This was the first I heard of it.

"Thank you very much." I could hardly contain myself.

"When I left Missouri, I brought Gregory's case with me, and I have been tracking it all this time."

All this time we were still trusting the Lord, but we thought it was still on hold, the Lord had people still working on Gregory's case. What a wonderful blessing that phone call was. He even gave me his direct line to his office.

We had to wait for a Parole hearing. When the day finally arrived, Gregory continued to maintain his innocence, which the parole board in any state does not like to hear. They want to see signs of contrition and Gregory had none because he did not commit the crime. He had sympathy for the family of the deceased but could not find it in himself, would not lie to himself, and did not satisfy the board by admitting to something he did not do. People who do not admit guilt do not get out on parole as a rule. The Parole Board considered the commutation and approved Gregory's parole.

I attended the parole hearing with him. One thing that any inmate needs is a home plan, well I was still driving a truck, so I did not have a home. That one situation cost Gregory 18 more months in prison until I got off the road and into the RV to establish a home plan for Gregory.

On Monday, June 11, 2007, I drove to the prison to pick Gregory up. I did not want him coming out dressed in ill-fitting state issue clothing, so I dropped off new clothes at the front office for him to change into when he left the prison. I sat out in my personal truck waiting for him. When I spied him walking out of prison, he was wearing his new clothes and looked handsome in them. He was carrying just one box of belongings with him. That summed up 22 years and 5 days of his life.

Would you believe our first stop was McDonald's for breakfast? I took a picture of him in his new civilian clothes, and he sent a picture to his brother on the new cell phone I had for him. Our next stop was my friend Fae's house for dinner and years of surprises. Through the years, for every Christmas and Birthday, I bought Gregory a present, and, on this day, he opened all his presents, which consisted of clothes, shoes, briefcase, new bible, and the list went on. It was an emotional time for all of us. Gregory said it was like going to be with the Lord and finding out all the good things He has in store for us when we go to be with Him.

CHAPTER 18
Algoa Correctional Center—The Release Center
by
Gregory

Algoa is one of the release centers for the Missouri Prison System and is the last facility that I went to before going to the street. It was built as a boys' school in 1932. There are 21 prisons in the state of Missouri with the headquarters in Jefferson City, Missouri, the state capital, and there are 2 release centers. Algoa was the one I was housed at until my release date of June 11, 2007. It was right across the street from Jefferson City Correctional Center JCCC the last maximum-security prison I was housed in. Once I was given a release date from the parole board, something that the state of Missouri said would never be, because of me having a life sentence running consecutively with a life sentence without the chance of probation and parole stipulation. I had to be transferred immediately to a level 2 camp from a level 5 facility. Level 2 is a minimum-security where level 5 is a maximum-security facility. According to the new laws in Missouri, a life sentence by itself carries 30 years and a life without parole and probation means that there is never any chance of me getting out of prison—EVER!

One of the questions that the governor's chief counsel asked me at a meeting we had at the prison was, "A life sentence is 30 years."

I told him, "When I was arrested it was near half that...thirteen to fifteen years...according to the law in Missouri then."

I think he said, "I have to check that out." The laws have changed over the years, and whatever law that I was under at that time would be the law that they would have to go by. One of the things I liked about the first governor's chief counsel is that he once told Bonnie, "We have to follow the law and we have to fight the law with the law. The law is like an onion, and you have to peel the layers off one by one." This is critical because the moment the governor said that I met the criteria of being innocent of the charges brought against me it showed his intent for my release—no one else could accost that. The Missouri Supreme Court has held this as a law that a governor's intent shall not be abridged, the State of Missouri v. Lute 2014. In the state, in accordance with the U. S. Constitution, we have the right to due process of law. I know a lot of times people in the legal profession want to pick and choose who they give liberty to and who they don't—that is not their choice. The law must be followed as the governor's chief counsel said.

I also had a chance to meet with the new administration's chief counsel and I don't know how he followed the law, but it appears his decisions may have been guided politically rather than legally and he felt that, seeing that I would be out of prison that was good enough. I didn't agree with this, but I knew at this point I would still be able to fight to clear my name.

I had an inmate tell me one time when he noticed how hard I had been fighting for my freedom, he said to me, "Greg, you might just have to accept black justice."

I whole heartly disagreed with him, because I said, "THERE IS NO SUCH THING!" Lady justice wears a blindfold for a reason. The only one that is peaking is us and this is where the problem comes in.

This same guy told me, "I am innocent too." I never doubted him, I prayed for him and he was released, and the state compensated him with 4.5 million dollars. Which I thought was a slap in the face for the years they took away from this young man's life. Money cannot compensate for that horrible time he spent; we will never know all the things that happened to him while in prison.

I have learned that we all have different battles to fight, some of them are harder than others and the Lord is no respecter of persons. Some injustice is treated differently because of the fear of those who do not want to be exposed; especially when it is going to affect their livelihood, and/or political ambitions. The trial judge in my case said it himself when he realized the slippery slope, they were on by using the statute 491.074. He stated, out of jury hearing range, "If the defense is correct [on the use of the statute 491.074] then we are in trouble." The two appeal courts said it was error [which proves it was a misuse of the law to which the governor's office rebukes the appeal courts for not taking it far enough and reversing the cases] ...but they called it harmless error. When dealing with people's lives—there is no harmless error. The error needs to be corrected.

What people fail to understand, is that not only did our framers of the Constitution set up rules to have due process of law, but within the framework of the due process we also have the right to a fair review. As you can see this is not what happened in my case.

This was an exciting time for me to be in the release center, because now I could see a light at the end of the tunnel. To occupy my time, I continued to go to church services and at times some of the men and I would go into the back-yard and put music to some of the songs I wrote while in prison. It was a joy to see the other men come out and listen as we performed the gospel music. I was singing one song acapella to a young man and he said that song convicted him and blessed him so much. What stood out to him was my voice being a perfect baritone voice unlike he has ever heard. I was looking forward to being on the outside with Bonnie a dream that had been long-awaited.

One of the other things I was able to do because the chaplain's clerk was being released and he asked the chaplain to replace his position with me. I was very humbled to be able to assist the chaplain in the many duties that he had in serving the inmates housed in Algoa. This gave me not only a job that I liked and enjoyed doing, but a step toward my calling. I was glad to be able to keep myself busy because you are in a release center the rules are much stricter and one thing can cause you to slip up and lose your out date. In my case I had to make sure that I kept my record spotless if I was going to be able to go out and clear my name. This also gave me the opportunity to learn a little bit about the computer. My wife would think I need to know a whole lot more—I agree.

I was housed here.

Algoa Correctional Center—The Release Center

CHAPTER 19
Our Legal Teams
by
Gregory & Bonnie

After we were able to secure a legal team that both Gregory and I agreed on, we sat back and let them work after I made sure they believed in Gregory's innocence. I knew that if they didn't believe in his innocence they would lack the effectiveness needed to defend Gregory. They told us their plan of attack they were going to pursue. They submitted letters to key places using the Freedom of Information Act. The one they heard back from first was the DEA. The DEA denied giving us any information pertaining to Andrew Chambers. Our lawyers told us they were going to appeal the rejection from the DEA. They petitioned the governor's archives and Probation and Parole for any information about the clemency, but they were told there were no records to be found, and that we had everything. They also petitioned the City of St. Louis for complete records. The response we got back surprised us. They declined—stating that the records are privileged information. In September 2014 our lawyer filed the first motion for a state Writ of Habeas Corpus for Actual Innocence and Manifest Injustice. We still didn't have any of the records from the governor's office, the city of St. Louis, or the DEA. It seemed that no one was cooperating with us at all.

Our lawyer sent us a copy of the brief. Both Gregory and I were pleasantly surprised. Everything we had told him was in the brief. "Greg," I asked. "Did the lawyer even study the case? This is as though we wrote it ourselves."

"He had to study it or he couldn't have put it together with the way he did. Did you notice that he used the word concocted when talking about the prosecutor's case against me?"

"Yes, I did. That is exactly what he did."

"I told you the Lord told me it was 'rigged!' That was a polite way of saying it."

It was a while before we received the counter brief from the AG's office. We couldn't believe it when we read it. Every point we were able to rebut. So, we put together a document where we rebutted every point the Assistant Attorney General (AAG) made.

Time went by and every motion that was made to get the records from St. Louis failed. Our lawyers had a shake-up in their office which caused much delay with moving our case forward. Our legal team had dwindled to one, but we knew he was brilliant and had won Writs before, so we hung in there. He submitted the case to a crime scene reenactor/forensic scientist who wrote an interesting report that in summation said, *In 40 years of investigating cases, I have never seen a prosecutor try to connect things that were not connectable and prove things that cannot be proven.* He then asked for the crime scene photos, which we had never seen before. Our lawyer was able to obtain the photos and sent us a copy. We were finally able to see the crime scene photos. It took 30 years but we had them in hand. After viewing them, there was no doubt that the prosecutor concocted a story against Greg. All of the blood evidence told a totally different story than the prosecutor told and those photos were never shown at trial. We couldn't believe that Gregory or Ronald's lawyer didn't bring them forward to refute the prosecutor's story. This is why even eyewitness testimony must be in line with forensic evidence or it means nothing.

Another issue that concerned me was in reference to Ronald's academic record. All through the trial, the prosecutor kept mocking Ronald's academic abilities or lack thereof. Not once did Ronald's defense lawyer issue any proof that Ronald indeed attended Kansas State University [KSU] thwarting the prosecution's accusations that he didn't go to college with the low IQ that he had. I believed that Ronald went to KSU and was studying Architecture because when I challenged him [not believing him myself] he knew all of the names of the personnel in the Architecture Department. In lieu of this, and because I am an alum of KSU I took it upon myself to call the registrar's office to see if I could get any legal documentation that would prove that Ronald was indeed a student at KSU then I could prove the deterioration in his cognition after the brain surgery. I let the registrar know that Ronald had died. She asked if we could make a trade. I would send her a copy of Ronald's death certificate so she could close out his file and she would send me a Certificate in good standing on Ronald which was legal but did not reveal any confidential information. Obtaining that information took a five-minute phone call yet Ronald's lawyer never took the time to do that. Another piece of evidence not secured by the defense.

After a couple of years, we received notification from our lawyer that he was closing his practice because of illness. Therefore, we had to find another lawyer that would follow through with what he began. Now we had a challenge on our hands, where were we going to begin our search for a new lawyer?

Gregory contacted a well-known lawyer that he helped put together a video reenactment. She was booked up but she had a referral for us so we set up an appointment. I put together a couple of binders to help explain as simply as possible Gregory's case to share with lawyers that we would interview. The first lawyer was a woman who had worked with our first lawyer before and she insulted him, which was a turn-off seeing we really respected him.

We didn't have a second choice yet, then one day Gregory told me of a legal team that was recommended to him. So I gave them a call. The lawyers were former Public Defenders who had gone to school together, one had served in St. Louis and the other worked in Kansas City. They both wanted to go into private practice so they set up an office in Kansas City, MO, and were licensed to practice both sides of the state line. We had already paid our previous lawyer in full and we would get nothing back. We just wanted them to pick up where our previous lawyer left off. I told them we could get them up to par in an eight-hour meeting. They insisted it would take at least 40 hours of study. When we met with them in person, both Gregory and I liked them. This was going to be another expensive proposition, but we just had to make it work.

We had several meetings with our new lawyers Josh and Garrett and I was thankful that Gregory studied the law as much as he did. Josh always seemed to play the devil's advocate at our meetings, but Gregory was always able to come back with solid answers that could be supported with law. Sometimes they would banter back and forth. When Gregory was able to make a solid point then Josh would back off. We wondered just how well he knew the case. We knew that Garrett knew the case, but he was usually quiet during our meetings only occasionally would he speak up, and usually that was to agree with Greg.

Our legal team requested documentation again to see if they would have any luck obtaining any more information. Several months after they started working on the case we were pleasantly surprised with what they came up with. In California, years earlier a Public Defender is the one who obtained the DEA files on Andrew Chambers and exposed his undercover activity with the DEA. Our lawyers had a good conversation with him and he was pleased to see that his work was still helping others. He sent the DEA file to our lawyers and they sent us a copy of it. There was a lot of redaction in it but almost all of the redaction was agent names. Chamber's activities for the years he had been working for the DEA was very obvious even the times that the DEA got him out of trouble were listed. What a gold mine of information we had. It had dates and places etc. This find really impressed Gregory and I.

Another great move from our new legal team was when they went to San Diego to depose the original prosecutor on Gregory's case. What a wealth of information they got from him. Even though he continued to say he couldn't remember a lot. He admitted that he remembered the DEA had some involvement in this case. Also, he proved himself to have played a part in suborn perjury along with failure to disclose evidence of relative and jury relationships. All of this being enough to reverse the case. After the deposition, the Assistant Attorney General who was present was so confused that he stated to our lawyers, " I have to find something bad against Gregory."

Shortly after the deposition, our lawyers contacted us to let us know that the Parole and Probation released to the Assistant Attorney General all the governor's records pertaining to the study of Gregory's case. Records we had been trying to get for years, but could not obtain. In the records, it was clear that Gregory had proven his innocence and that neither the court nor appeal court did right by Greg. The governor's notes even rebuked the appeal court in Gregory's case.

One of the clearest statements in the record was that the governor's office stated "the worst thing that Gregory **might** be guilty of is a misdemeanor that **might** have carried a one year jail sentence." When our lawyers saw this they were infuriated and wrote the Assistant Attorney General a memo asking him to just give in. He said he couldn't without asking his boss. His boss was mad when he found out that he gave the records to our lawyers and he, in turn, asked our lawyers to destroy the evidence that he had just given them and not to give us the information. This is a federal offense.

We had so much new evidence to present for the Writ of Habeas Corpus it is unthinkable to think that the judge would do anything but the right thing and grant us the writ. We had to first; get him to admit into the record all of the new evidence we discovered. Second was to get the judge to look seriously at the merits of the case, which it appears he didn't. It appears to us that someone convinced the judge to not allow us the Writ because the Assistant Attorney General made the statement in court, "judge, this case does not have the public outcry that would warrant you the exception of the moot issue." He also asked the judge to put a protective order on the evidence from the governor's office which was apparent that they were afraid of and didn't want the media to get ahold of it.

During the time that the Writ was in the court, my wife had to make an emergency move to Michigan to take care of her 100-year-old mother and sister who had 4th stage Parkinson's. I asked permission of the Probation and Parole

Office to transfer my case to Michigan. When Michigan accepted the case they asked for the documentation around my case so they would know who they were dealing with.

By

Bonnie

Before Gregory even met with his Michigan Parole Officer, He received a phone call from his officer and she told me that she had never seen a state do what Missouri just did. They took him off Parole and refused to send the paperwork to Michigan. Then Missouri said his case was moot. According to federal law, the state can't call for mootness in the middle of the case if they are the ones who created it. That law evidently didn't get to Missouri courts and the judge chose to accept the additional lie from the Attorney General's office and the mootness issue instead of reviewing the merits of the case. Consequently, despite all the evidence, the judge ruled our argument moot and that was the final step in the state court. Gregory will never quit until his name is cleared somehow.

CHAPTER 20
I Have to Clear My Name
by
Gregory

When Bonnie met with the head of Probation and Parole, he advised her on what we needed to do. His concern was to get me out of prison and then work to clear my name. For me to digest this the Lord had to speak a word to me. It was around the time that He told me, "Gregory I sometimes move in steps and stages." Years later I heard a preacher preach a sermon on a similar subject, confirming the Word He spoke to me. As I matured more in the Word, I noticed that when the Lord performs an instant miracle and gives us what we desire right then and there, then we rarely gain anything from it. Or, should I say, we get what we desire and not a lesson within. When the Lord moves in steps and stages, we get more than we desire. And we learn a great lesson along the way. I am not saying it is easy, but as we see the many disciples going through fires, trials, and tribulations; they came out on the other side with great testimonies that help us even to this day.

It is exciting to see the Lord at work and perform miracles, but just like the Israelites when they were delivered from Egypt, they saw many miracles, yet they continued to doubt God. When it was time for them to enter the Promised

Land, only two had the type of faith that was pleasing to God. Joshua and Caleb said they could do it—they could possess the land. For us to get in a posture of "walking free" we must have the God type of faith to do it.

✚

*"**A good name** is to be chosen rather than **great** riches, loving favor rather than silver and gold."* (Proverbs 22:1)

When your name is heard what do people do? They associate you with one thing or another. Emotionally I could not allow my name to be associated with a lie, and just because they chose to build one lie on top of another lie. That does not make it right. My name will still be associated with it. As one of my attorneys said, "a lie is a lie no matter the subject." As the old saying goes, "you can put lipstick on a pig, but it is still a pig." The Apostle Paul was thrown in prison and the guards wanted to throw him out privately. Although I am a citizen of Heaven my earthly citizenship is in America, which those rights are not suspended me because someone thinks they should be. For the state to try and hide these things in my case and not allow my name to be cleared is just as bad as what was done to the Apostle Paul and Silas.

And when it was day, the magistrates sent the serjeants, saying, Let those men go. And the keeper of the prison told this saying to Paul, The magistrates have sent to let you go: now therefore depart, and go in peace. But Paul said unto them, They have beaten us openly uncondemned, being Romans, and have cast us into prison; and now do they thrust us out privily? nay verily; but let them come themselves and fetch us out. And the serjeants told these words unto the magistrates: and they feared, when they heard that they were Romans. And they came and besought them, and brought them out, and desired them to depart out of the city. And they went out of the prison, and entered into the house of Lydia: and when they had seen the brethren, they comforted them, and departed. (Acts 16 35-40)

We can see from the Scriptures the Lord does not desire for us to allow our good to be evil spoken of. Nor does he want us to allow mistreatment to be done to us and the people who inflict it to go without consequence or correction. The magistrate in the scripture feared when they realized when Paul relied on his Roman citizenship, and they had beaten them openly not being condemned. The reason these men feared was because they truly respected the Roman law and knew it was unlawful to mistreat a Roman citizen for no just cause. I respect them for that because they did not make up a reason, nor lie about it, nor concoct stories to try and find a way to harm God's Apostles. It is a crime to flog a Roman citizen; to flog him is wickedness; to put him to death is almost parricide.[i] Just as well it is a crime that was done in the Oliver case and there is no way around that except to correct the wrong as the Romans did for Paul and Silas.

I was meditating one day, and the Lord impressed on my heart that what the governor's office was attempting to do was trying to fix the problem yet not fixing it because my name is not yet clear. When Adam and Eve sinned against God, Adam tried to fix the problem and sewed fig leaves to hide their nakedness. The Lord let them know that this was not suitable to cover the sin, but as a temporary provision, the Lord provided a suitable covering until he brought the true solution.

All this was to get us to understand that there is a right and wrong way to do things because my name should not carry, ex-felon of a crime I did not commit. The stigma that man tries to put on you is not who you really are. Although his attempt is to discredit you for some reason or another, rather than take the time to really get to know you. This is something that happens too often in our society. We all are different and have likes and dislikes, but the true freedom we do have is to choose to get to know our neighbors whenever the chance arises. I have learned over the years with being around over 5,000 men in a close environment that you can learn things about people that you ordinarily wouldn't learn.

CHAPTER 21

The Businessman

by

Gregory

Another promise the Lord made to me was that He was going to put me back in business. Before I was arrested, the business that I was running was called, "Handy Person Co." The type of work was a service for cleaning supermarkets and general commercial businesses. I also did some moving and hauling and sub-contracting work was one of the ways I would fill my contracts.

Once I was released from prison, I started walking the street to put in application after application with no success. It became apparent that this was some of the collateral damage this conviction had caused me. It was affecting every area of my life. I could not give up though. I continued to ride the bus and walk the street whatever I could do. The job service the system led me to was a joke I did everything they told me to do to no avail. I finally found a part-time job at a truck stop filling station and I explained to them that I spent 22 years in prison for crimes I did not commit. I also wanted them to know that I had good work ethics. The owner said, "I'm going to give you a chance." I started out working the midnight shift after I was trained. I really liked the work. I was a cashier, stocker, and nighttime clean-up. I was honored that they trusted me with their money and their store. It was wonderful being free to make money for myself and to start trying to live again. I worked it for quite a while until they had to cut hours for everyone. This was sad because my wife had bought me a truck before I got out and the distance that this was would not make it feasible to continue. I had to find something else. So, I started looking all over again. It just so happened right across the street from where we lived was an Italian Sausage factory that I stopped in to see if they were hiring. I was always upfront with people and let them know I had been in prison. When the owner heard my story, he didn't have any work in the factory, but he had a mobile food cart that he was going to allow me to work in the downtown area in Kansas City. I had never done anything like this before and I told him I hadn't but I knew how to cook. He said, "That's Okay. I am going to put you out there with another guy and he will train you." I had to go to the Health Department and take a class to get my food handler's certificate. I was excited because this was something different.

Once I had gotten everything that was needed, I was ready to go. He forgot to tell me that the man who worked the cart before me had gone downtown and worked the cart without a permit. This created a problem with the Health Department because all vendors must be permitted. I really wanted to do this so I wound up going to the Health Department with the cart to get it permitted. Little did I know it was going to take us months to get the permit because once that cart was flagged the Health Department continued to find every excuse, they could not pass the cart. I was determined to see this through, but it wasn't doing my wife and I any good on the financial side. Until I could bring in revenue, he couldn't afford to pay me. He finally came to the Health Department with me, and we went over the inspector's head to his boss and the boss said "What is the problem?"

We explained to him, "We felt our cart is being flagged because someone had worked it previously without a permit." I just wanted to do it right and follow the law.

So, the boss told the inspector, "Give them another inspection date and if they have the things, you told them was wrong with it fixed...pass it" So that is what happened, and we passed just in time to catch some of the events at the Sprint Center. This was a nice deal in a way because he had a van to pull the cart and I would take it down to the Sprint Center when they had events and in front of his girlfriend's office when the Sprint Center didn't have any events. His factory specialized in making Italian Sausage. So the purpose of all this was to promote his product. He had even gotten his line of sausage into several grocery stores during this season. They had been in business for over 60 years as a neighborhood supplier. So here I was getting a chance to function like a sub-contractor for an existing company. Which would give me experience. As long as I sold the product, he gave me the run of things, so I cooked the sausage from a St. Louis style the way my mom taught me how to do it. As the people were going to and from the Sprint Center, they would stop and order the Italian sausage, a pop and chips. What drew them was the smell of the sausage cooking with the green peppers and onions seasoned the Italian way along with spaghetti sauce. Everything was working well for a while. I was making a little money but not much although I enjoyed what I was doing.

One night I had to get up inside the van to get some utensils and I noticed a blue money bag tucked away inside the van wall. I sensed I had to look in it to see if the owner had left a bag of money in the van and forgot it. To my surprise, it was a 38 caliber Beretta semi-automatic pistol. I was furious because I was on papers. How could I have explained that to the police if they had pulled me over for any reason? I took the van and everything back to him and let him know about the gun and that it put me at risk. He treated it like it was nothing, but I had to tell him, "No, this could cost me prison time for a parole violation."

When he understood how angry I was he apologized and said, "That will never happen again. The other guy must have forgotten to take it out and he kept it in the van in case of robbery."

We got another opportunity to promote the sausage at a Kansas City Dragstrip. They raced cars, dragsters, and motorcycles. They let me set my cart up and they didn't allow me to sell anything but Italian sausage at first. They let us in to buffer the crowd because they had five vending buildings and they needed extra help. On one Sunday, we broke all records, and that afternoon we sold over $1000 in Italian Sausage. No soda, no water, no chips. It was a miracle we were able to do that. This also boosted the sausage company's name. It wasn't long that the man in charge of the racetrack wanted to bring me in independently from the sausage company, because we made such a hit. For me to do that I had to have my own cart.

My wife's son made it possible for us to get a stainless-steel enclosed cart 8'X 16' with three operating windows. I had to go and speak to the owner of the sausage company to let him know I was going into business for myself. At first, he felt like I was abandoning him, but then he realized this was a good opportunity for me. I explained to him we still could use his sausage so he wouldn't be losing money on that. This turned out to be a wonderful deal because as soon as I started working the track, the owner of the track asked me how much I was paying for the sausage. He paid me that amount and then he paid to stock whatever I bought and all he asked for was 35% of sales. What a deal that was and we were really making a name for ourselves around there. The motorcycle gang made sure that all their people bought from us. I forgot when I first went to the track that I told a young man that we were going to get a stand-in cook unit. He didn't forget, when he saw us, he told all his friends, "You are going to buy from him!" Then there were quite a few people who started buying Italian sausage.

Another business venture that I had secured was a contract with Swift Transportation, the largest full truckload carrier in the country. I tried to get a job with them when I first got out of prison, but when Swift sent my records to their legal department, I was turned down because of the conviction the state had put on me. I was skilled as a diesel mechanic from the military and that job would have been a great opportunity for my wife and I to get ahead. Both the terminal manager and the shop manager went to bat for me but legal didn't budge. I then came up with the idea of detailing the big rigs. Bonnie told me to talk to management, but to keep her out of it because she wanted nothing to do with a potential conflict of interest seeing she worked for Swift. Therefore, that is what I did. After a bit of negotiation and getting the necessary insurance for the business, Swift approved my proposal and I started detailing their trucks. One day the restaurant owner in the Swift Terminal went on vacation leaving all the employees without food nearby. I asked the Terminal Manager if I could cook for them while he was gone. They approved it. We cleared over $1500 that week in cooking alone.

Eventually, we moved the big unit on the premises and became a fixture. Our hours did not conflict with the restaurant hours. We always waited until he was closed before we opened because we did not want to affect his business. So, at this time I was detailing trucks, running a mobile restaurant, and snow plowing. My brother bought me a plow blade for the truck Bonnie bought me. I thank the Lord for Bonnie and all who assisted in some way to make my life a bit easier since the state tried to ruin it.

I had to go to parole meetings once a week at first and pay $30 per month to be out on parole. My parole officer once asked me, "How did you start a mobile restaurant business/"

I told her, "I am who I am, I am a businessman and not who the world thinks I am."

Once the Swift contract was rolling well. I did some more cold calling and landed the same type of contract with Knight Transportation. Only with Knight I also cleaned the showers and the building. They also gave me decal removal on their trailers when they were getting ready for sale. This opened doors for other companies that needed the same type of work done. MHC which is Kenworth also gave me business occasionally. My snowplow contracts were companies like O'Reilly's, Shell filling stations, Truck Insurance Company and these people did not want anyone else touching their property once I did it.

By this time, I was employing others to help me carry the load. I had a couple of full-time people at Knight and one full-time person at Swift. I also got a contract with Swift at Walmart and had an employee work that contract every other week. I was the backup person for Swift and Knight when we got busy. I was glad to get workers on board because until then I couldn't take a break or vacation time at all. Bonnie took care of my bookwork and she noticed that the company increased $20,000 every year, which we know was truly God's blessing.

Unfortunately, my legs were suffering from the deformity that was caused by a military injury and it was continuing to get worse. It restricted me from doing the work like I used to do and I had to hire as many people as I could to accomplish the job. This really cut deep into our profitability. I was glad to be able to help others, but as much as has been taken from us over the years we needed the help. I just had to continue to trust the Lord for our provisions. I learned that when you are dealing with large companies it takes time for invoices to be paid. That put an additional strain on us because I paid my workers on time whether we got paid or not. I had to set up bank buffers to make sure my people were paid on time because sometimes it was months before we got invoices cleared up.

Thou shalt not defraud thy neighbour, neither rob him: the wages of him that is hired shall not abide with thee all night until the morning. (Leviticus 19:13)

Unfortunately, Bonnie had to go back to Michigan to take care of her 100-year-old mother and sister who had advanced-stage Parkinson's Disease. She was able to work out of the house full time and keep her job at Swift. Because of this, I asked the Probation and Parole for an emergency transfer to Michigan. Consequently, I had to get rid of my contracts, and fortunately, I was able to sell one due to the immediate transfer. Michigan approved my transfer, but they asked Missouri for my files so they would know who they were supervising. Missouri refused to turn over the files, because they knew what was in them and, because the transfer was in motion they immediately took me off papers.

CHAPTER 22
An Old Army Injury
by
Gregory

After I got out of prison, the first thing Bonnie had me do was to get a thorough physical and a dental exam, because for over 20 years I received little to no medical or dental attention. By that time I had spent 22 years and five days in prison the old injury had worked on my body, my legs were deformed from an old injury I received while I was stationed by the DMZ in Korea. I received the injury shortly before I was finished with my second tour of the service. One night Bonnie had to rush me to the ER because of the pain I was experiencing in my ankle and foot. It was at my follow-up visit with my internist that he found in my X-rays the old ankle injury I received in Korea. He saw a chip in my ankle bone and realized that the gout I was experiencing came from that old injury. With this information, I went to the VA hospital in Kansas City, MO. They looked at my X-rays and my medical record and told me I had a sprained ankle. I could not figure out how a sprained ankle could last 30 years. I went to a civilian foot specialist to get a second opinion and he could not believe what he saw in my ankle. He was shocked that the Army had not taken an MRI of my ankle to see exactly what was going on and what cause my deformity.

Little did I know this was going to lead me into another battle on a different front. I had to file a claim for a service-connected injury. I joined the US Army in 1975, and I initially was a diesel mechanic. My M.O.S. (Military Occupational Code) was 63 H.

When I reenlisted after my first tour of duty, I changed my M.O.S. to 26 Delta. For this enlistment, I was a Radar Technician for tactical and fixed radar. My injury happened when I was assigned to Seoul, Korea. In Seoul, our job was to support the 2nd Division whose job it was to protect the DMZ. It was important for our unit to stay in top physical condition. Instead of running and doing PT the normal way we did what they called Combat Physical Training, which was much more strenuous. This is how I incurred my injury. After I got out of the Army, four years later is when I got arrested and wound up in prison. My time in prison compounded the effects of my injury, because of the lack of medical treatment.

I was fighting the system on two fronts. I was fighting to right the wrongful imprisonment on the judicial side and I was fighting the VA for a claim of a missed diagnosis of an injury on another side. The missed diagnoses on my ankle compounded with lengthy wrongful incarceration—caused my legs and feet to eventually become deformed because my gait was off. After the VA finally gave me an MRI, they discovered that I had been walking around on a trabecular microfracture and chronically torn ligament for over 30 years. It was not until the MRI proved that they missed the diagnosis in Korea that I was able to get proper treatment. Finally, after 10 years of fighting the VA, I was able to get both of my knees replaced over a period of four years. Fighting the VA seemed to be a never-ending process, but with the grace of God, I was able to receive the proper benefits and get my legs repaired.

Not only will I be "Walking Free," in general, but I will be "Walking Free" with straight legs having the spring back in my step as I had as a young man. Praise the Lord!

CHAPTER 23
The Deposition
by
Gregory & Bonnie

Originally, we had a hearing for the state Writ of Habeas Corpus scheduled for September 2018, but our lawyers wanted to depose of the original prosecutor, Garrett Randall, about the case. He was now retired. We didn't know what to expect; most likely it would be a bunch of legal ease talking round in circles spinning every answer to his favor like politicians do never admitting to any wrongdoing. We paid for our lawyers to fly to San Diego, California for the deposition. The Assistant Attorney General also flew there on the state's nickel. They all met at Mr. Randall's home, the three attorneys and a court reporter to make it official.

We were confident with how our lawyer Garrett would handle the questioning of Mr. Randall, but we were not sure about Josh. Gregory and Josh always seemed to spar with each other. Josh kept saying he did not know the case as well as Garrett, and that was true from all appearances. The deposition was held on my 74th birthday. I began working on Gregory's case when I was 42 years old. The 32 years just seemed to drag by with one postponement after another. Another way the legal system works is to ware people down until they just give up. We were not sure what the deposition would yield us, but we were sure hoping Mr. Randall would reveal the truth as we knew it and...could prove it.

After the deposition, our lawyers contacted us and let us know that they had some good stuff, especially about the DEA. That made our day and we couldn't wait to get a copy of the deposition. Because we knew the case so well, we knew we would see more than just the information about the DEA that was incriminating. We were on pins and needles waiting for our copy of the transcript to arrive. It took a couple of weeks, but our lawyers finally emailed us a copy of the deposition. I printed out a copy right away and spent the evening studying it. Gregory only got part of the way through it before he went to work. I had my trusty yellow highlighter in hand as I went through it. Right out of the gate our lawyers asked Mr. Randal about his boss, George Peach who got disbarred for misappropriation of government funds and other activities he participated in while he was the St. Louis DA. Mr. Randall admitted that he handled the fund that Mr. Peach stole from and he gave him the charge card that he embezzled from.

by
Gregory

There is another story about Mr. Peach that gave a motive for what happened at my trial. While Ronald and I were still at City Jail [1985-1987], my grandfather pretended to be J.B. "Jet" Banks senate majority leader of the state legislature on the phone and called Mr. Peach. When he got through to Mr. Peach, he told him he wasn't "Jet" Banks and that he was Harry Harris, Ronald's, and my granddad. He preceded to tell Mr. Peach about Ronald's mental condition and my innocence and begged for justice and fairness for us. Mr. Peach's response set in motion the actions that took over 30 years of investigation to uncover. "Mr. Harris," Mr. Peach said, "because you have done this to me, I will see to it that neither one of your grandsons ever see the light of day." Mr. Randal was second in command at the District Attorney's Office and was assigned Ronald's and my cases. That was the beginning of the concocted story that the state built against me and in essence Ronald too.

To sum up what came out of the state's deception was that there were two un-endorsed witnesses, which equates to suborn perjury. To make this revelation more important, was Josh who was doing some of the questioning and the way he questioned him. We discovered that Josh's style was to back snakes into the corner and then not give them a chance to strike back. He just backs the snakes in the corner and cuts off their head so they can't strike back. What also surprised us was how well prepared and well-versed Josh was in the case. All those sparring sessions I had with Josh were causing him to get a solid foundation, also he could see how hard I could push back with the law behind me. One thing that one must do when battling the law is to know the law well enough to fight back with law. You cannot fight the law with emotion. Both my lawyers found out that I really knew the law around my case, and I was even able to teach them a few things.

The AAG had sent Mr. Randall a full copy of the case record for him to review before the deposition so he could refresh his memory. Based on the way he answered the questions he obviously didn't study the case because he conveniently forgot a lot of things or was he trying to rely on plausible deniability like so many politicians do? He couldn't do that because it was his notes that exposed much of the exculpatory evidence we obtained.

One of the answers to a question surprised us. He remembered the DEA's involvement in this case but was unclear as to why they were involved. He could not remember why he nolle prose the charges for the shooting of Andrew Chambers...the DEA's highest-paid narcotics snitch. We knew why! The DEA did not want Chambers to get exposed in any way for what he was doing for the DEA. So, they secreted him away in a temporary pseudo witness protection program so he would not be available for trial. At court, Mr. Randall just said that they could not find Andrew Chambers. Because of the nolle pros, any evidence that this second eyewitness had was lost. In his deposition was proof that I had no knowledge of what my mentally impaired brother was going to do. In any case...there was no necessary intent that they call 'mens rea' present in my case and Andrew Chambers was the proof of that. In his deposition, he had exculpatory evidence that stated that I was yelling at my brother telling him "What is you doing? You can't go shooting people!" Which is called excited utterance and proved that I had no knowledge of what my brother was going to do. Because of the DEA protecting Andrew Chambers...this truth about my case never came out.

Our lawyers went on to show him notes that were discovered indicating that he knew full well that the relationship between the deceased and the witness-at-large, Ernest Fields who was the unendorsed ringer hearsay on hearsay witness. In the judge's 19-page memorandum justifying his decision to uphold the jury decision he held Ernest Fields in high esteem justifying his decision to uphold the jury decision, Ernest Fields had a horrible, uninformed testimony...and why anyone believed him was beyond comprehension. This relationship we discovered was kept from the defense. There were two unendorsed witnesses one police officer and Ernest Fields, both gave false testimony, but were allowed to do so based upon the fact that the case was tried on an illegal statute 491-074, which allowed for hearsay testimony and gave leverage for overzealous prosecutors and police to fabricate evidence.

Next, it was time for the AAG to question Mr. Randall. All he could do was to try and save the integrity of the case by asking a question like, "you didn't mean to do this or that...." Of course, his answer was that he didn't do anything maliciously wrong. After the deposition, the AAG told our lawyers that he had to find something against me because the deposition proved to be against the state's approach to my case. That is when the AAG got a hold of the governor's paperwork. This was paperwork we had been asking for years, and that the Probation and Parole Office refused to give us. They covered it up by telling our lawyers that they had sent everything. The Freedom of Information Act went totally out the window in my case. The AAG sent the governor's paperwork to my lawyers as he would any discovery information. Once my lawyers read it, they were hot and immediately contacted the AAG and asked him to just drop the case and surrender because the governor's records were damning to the state. He told them he had to get with his boss first, he could not just do it unilaterally. When he got back with my lawyers, he let them know that his boss was mad and that he was not supposed to give them that information. Then he asked them to destroy some of the governor's notes and not to let us know about it. My lawyers were cussing mad and told him that they would not destroy this information pertaining to their clients. It was too late, I already had a copy of the governor's notes and I also received a copy of the email where the AAG was asking my lawyers to destroy the information.

On Sun, Jan 20, 2019 at 2:22 PM Goodwin, Gregory wrote:

183

Dear Counsel:

I am writing this e-mail following our telephone conversation from the afternoon of January 19, 2019, and I have included Caroline Coulter, my supervisor. In the conversation, we discussed your client's parole file, which I provided to you the afternoon of January 18, 2019. In our conversation, you mentioned a few documents: the Board of Probation and Parole's Executive Clemency Summary and Recommendation dated September 30, 2004, as well as a draft version of that documents, in addition to some e-mails. When I reviewed the parole file before providing it to you, I did not realize those documents, or the memorandum dated February 11, 1998, or the memorandum dated October 29, 2003, were included in the file. That was my mistake.

Those documents are privileged and were inadvertently disclosed. Missouri Statutes indicate the records in the Probation and Parole file that are created by a member or employee of the Board is a privileged record. Section 549.500. Some of these documents also constitute attorney-client privilege or work product. In a previous conversation, I had indicated that the Cole County Circuit Court's position in another case was that an offender's attorney could have access to the offender's file during discovery. That did not extend to the above captioned documents, which total 37 pages. Because the disclosure of these documents was inadvertent, the privilege has not been waived. **We request that you return or destroy these documents and any copies of them immediately.**

I apologize for the inconvenience that this has caused.
Sincerely,
Gregory M. Goodwin
Assistant Attorney General

Our Lawyers response; Date: Sun, Jan 20, 2019, at 5:14 PM

Dear Counsel

I hope you understand that we are deeply troubled that there are documents which strongly support our position, and that you are now asking for them to be destroyed / hidden. That being said, I am sure you can appreciate that on behalf of our client, we cannot agree to this without an order from the court.

There was no order from the court. As a matter of fact, the AAG asked the court not to allow this evidence into the hearing as evidence. To which the judge stated, "We don't have secrets here." Because of that the files the state wanted to be destroyed are now public records.

CHAPTER 24
Intellectual v. Spiritual
by
Gregory

The intellectual world believes that it is education that is the key to unlocking the door to success, and for the most part, there is some truth in that. It does, however, limit the individual to the endless possibilities that awaits them in achieving "good success." If we are going to be *"Walking Free,"* we need to learn the difference between intellectual knowledge and spiritual knowledge.

There are two types of wisdom in this world; there is spiritual wisdom and worldly wisdom. The scriptures tell us that

This wisdom [worldly] *is not that which comes down from above, but is earthly, natural, demonic. For where jealousy and selfish ambition exists there is disorder in every evil thing. But the wisdom from above is first pure, then peaceable, gentle, reasonable, full of mercy, good fruits, unwavering without hypocrisy."* (*James 3:15-17 NASB*)

Growing up in the inner city of St. Louis, Missouri, I learned there was a certain standard that was pushed down the throats of many of the young blacks at an early age. "Get a good education, work hard and it will open many doors for you." That sounds good, doesn't it? The problem is I realized that this is a cop-out for many of those searching minds looking for the true meaning in life and purpose. Seeing that we live in a microwave society, religion, and everything else pertaining to moral values and that way of life is just piled on top of this flippant ideology. This may anger a lot of people because they will think that I am attacking education, but really, I am attacking worldly wisdom. This ideology was so ingrained in my family life that it was almost impossible to escape making it harder for me to be 'walking free' in the truth of the Word of God.

Although it is good advice to get an education there is also another dynamic at work in our inner cities which undermines any sound advice or reasoning that could have come from these parents and teachers. For example, my father who was from the old school of thought still had a bit of the slave mentality seeing he was from the deep South, Mississippi being born shortly after the turn of the 20th century. Because my father was 37 years older than my mother, consequently, his influence was only able to reach myself and the older siblings, five brothers, and one sister. I am the oldest of the union between my mother and father. We were blessed to be raised in a two-parent household and my father was a businessman and preacher, and my mother taught us the Word of God. My father had children from a previous union all of which are deceased except for one daughter. My mother was from Tennessee and was the oldest of nine siblings and often had to care for her younger brothers and sisters.

I remember the TV show that I use to watch as a child. "Rich Man Poor Man" was about two brothers. They both had the same opportunities but went in totally different directions. It seemed the rich brother always was trying to do things to help the other brother, but because they had opposing ideologies it made it impossible for them to have a normal relationship. Another thing that is prevalent in the black community is; when someone becomes successful, he/she is looked upon as the champion of the community. Others become jealous and they try to pull them back into where they came from like "crabs in a barrel syndrome" making it difficult for the successful person to reach back and lift their suffering community out of a way of thinking that has plagued them for so long. We saw this played out when Bill Cosby tried to get the youth to change their appearance, language, music lyrics, and lifestyle that stereotypes the average black American youth. He was laughed at and mocked and considered old fashion, but Bill Cosby although, not without his own moral problems, is a perfect example of what education and hard work can do for someone. He was just trying to get the black community to see the reality of what his basic training brought him. Even though many rappers today tapped into a billion-dollar industry, it is shaping the culture in such a way to degrade women and disrespect oneself. Success in the world's eye is seen by money, material things, and status. Where 'good success' is gauged by the purity of mind, heart, and spirit of a person, and the completeness of one lacking nothing, but is *"Walking Free"* in a world filled with confusion, power struggles, and deception all around. This helps put life in the right perspective where the Lord has lifted an individual to the level of understanding that is able to take the education, moral values, and hard work and use them for kingdom purposes and not selfish gain.

My point in all of this is that I had to realize that while many were in their worldly universities I was in the University of the Lord Jesus Christ, which allowed me to learn about the two schools of thought and the good old cliché began to make sense, which is 'get a good education, work hard and it will open up doors for you.' As I grew in my understanding of the Lord, I learned that it was He who was the door to the understanding of what I had learned and what I was really looking for. In His Word, is where I found it. He says:

I am the way the truth and the life, no man cometh to the Father but by me. (John 14: 6)

It is not religion that taught me this, not some guru, or some ideology—No...it is my personal, intimate relationship with the Lord that helped me to see that we all can be 'walking-free.'

Ask yourself;

- Are you bound to anything? You can be 'walking free.
- Are you trapped in bad thinking? You can be 'walking-free.'
- Are people trying to control you? You can be 'walking-free.'
- Are you suffering from depression? You can be 'walking-free.'
- Has your family let you down? You can be 'walking-free.'
- Has a loved one failed to listen to your sound advice? You can be 'walking-free.'
- Does stinking thinking from past events have you bound? You can be 'walking-free.'

Whatever the situation you are facing...you...can be 'walking-free!'

In our society, we rely on experts, (the learned intellectual) to solve every problem we face. For the most part, some of them have some good ideas but are rarely able to solve any of the problems. At the end of the discussions, it usually winds up being another chance to "throw money" at the problem. Money is not the cure-all for the problem, but many experts use it in promoting their projects and books that are filled with worldly wisdom. If you have a problem to solve you would not throw money at it because that doesn't solve anything and never gets to the root of the problem. You work the problem, develop a solution, create the formula until you have an answer. I had to learn that I do not have a problem, that is right I will say it again I do not have a problem. When the Lord comes into your life and makes you free you do not have a problem you have the problem solver in your life. The problem is many of God's people do not know the treasures that lie within them, and that lack of knowledge keeps them bound up and incapable of "*Walking Free.*"

> "*My people are destroyed for a lack of knowledge: because thou hast rejected knowledge, I will also reject thee, that thou shalt be no priest to me: seeing thou hast forgotten the law of thy God, I will also forget thy children.*" (Hosea 4:1 KJV)

The word of God is full of wisdom and only God's Word can make one wise unto Salvation. Being in the University of Jesus Christ I have learned many great and valuable lessons. If we are going to be "*Walking Free*" all the Lord's children need to realize is that there is a problem but knowing how to solve it can be a dilemma if we lean on our own understanding. The solution, however, comes through his only begotten Son Jesus Christ of Nazareth. Some might have a problem understanding the solution as to what ails them and understanding the solution at work. The root of our problems is sin and has been since the fall of man and the only solution is God's perfect sacrifice Jesus Christ. Once He is in our hearts and life there is no room for the enemy to have place.

Jesus said it best *"... the prince of this world cometh, and hath nothing in me."* (John 14:30)

What a profound statement the Lord made here:

If we are going to live an overcoming life, then Jesus is our best example, and wouldn't it be nice if we can say as Jesus did that the enemy has nothing in us. When the problem solver lives big on the inside there is no problem without a solution. And we become *"More than Conquerors"* with the Lord!

> *"Nay, in all these things we are more than conquerors through him that loved us.*
>
> *For I am persuaded, that neither death, nor life, nor angels, nor principalities, nor powers, nor things present, nor things to come,*
>
> *Nor height, nor depth, nor any other creature, shall be able to separate us from the love of God, which is in Christ Jesus our Lord."* (Romans 8:37-39)

CHAPTER 25

The Writ of Habeas Corpus Hearing

by

Gregory

Habeas corpus, an ancient common-law writ, issued by a court or judge directing one who holds another in custody to produce the person before the court for some specified purpose. Although there have been and are many varieties of the writ, the most important it is that used to correct violations of personal liberty by directing judicial inquiry into the legality of a detention. The habeas corpus remedy is recognized in the countries of the Anglo-American legal system but is generally not found in civil law countries, although some of the latter have adopted comparable procedures.

The origins of the writ cannot be stated with certainty. Before the Magna Carta (1215) a variety of writs performed some of the functions of habeas corpus. During the Middle Ages habeas corpus was employed to bring cases from inferior tribunals into the king's courts. The modern history of the writ as a device for the protection of personal liberty against official authority may be said to date from the reign of Henry VII (1485–150) when efforts were made to employ it on behalf of persons imprisoned by the Privy Council. By the reign of Charles I, in the 17th century, the writ was fully established as the appropriate process for checking the *illegal imprisonment* of people by inferior courts or public officials.

Many of the procedures that made for the effective assertion of these rights were provided by the Habeas Corpus Act of 1679, which authorized judges to issue the writ when courts were on vacation and provided severe penalties for

Henry VII

any judge who refused to comply with it. Its use was expanded during the 19th century to cover those held under private authority. In 1960 legislation was enacted limiting the instances in which habeas corpus could be denied and establishing new lines of appeal.[ii]The Editors of Encyclopedia Britannica

When I initially started fighting to unravel this wrongful conviction, the Lord instructed me to study all types of law, Judeao, Mosaic, Old Common Day Law, the U.S. Constitution, and the Biblical Laws. This was to give me a solid foundation and an understanding of the inner workings of the legal process.

I remember when Bonnie and I had gone before the Probation and Parole Board Hearing. I explained to them that I was innocent, but because the courts had failed and dropped the ball, I had to pursue a justice avenue through clemency. It was interesting that when the board took note that I was maintaining my innocence one of the panel members said, "You know we are the Board?"

I responded, "Yes, I do."

Although I did not explain my reasoning to the panel member, I knew that in my heart of the heart that the Lord was using the board like the old Common Day Court to redress the illegality that took place in the courts that I went through to right the wrong that should have been done within the courts.

I was led to pursue my writ of Habeas Corpus and at this time I had been on parole for about seven years. To make sure that I was filling in the right venue, the Probation and Parole Board was that venue because I was still on papers and under their supervision. I didn't want to be wrong, but there are rules and procedures of law that one must follow. I had talked to my parole officer when I was released from prison and explained to her that because I am an innocent man I want to continue to fight to clear my name but I didn't want to overstep my authority. She told me, "You can do this as long as you obtain legal counsel." I chuckled because I knew my Parole Officer knew that Bonnie and I fought my case before the Governor's Office without legal counsel and secured my release.

As a believer I knew to not disrespect authority, therefore I sought out council and we found an attorney who knew how to fight this type of issue. It was he that helped us set the stage to not only get the ball rolling on the state Habeas Corpus but secure a hearing. Interestingly he was married to an attorney, so we were getting two for one and she too was very sharp. As a matter of fact, she gave me some law that the court has tried to duck and that is law on the "moot-ness issue." What the mootness issue deals with is that courts try to say that your claim is moot if you are not in prison or under supervision, but the U.S. Federal Courts have long held that as long as there are collateral issues then there is an exception to the mootness issue. Because I was on papers the Federal Court also holds that you are still perceived as being incarcerated because you are under supervision.

HABEAS STANDARD

This Court has the authority to "issue and determine original remedial writs," including writs of habeas corpus. Mo. Const. art. V, sec. 14. Section 532.010 RSMo states, "Every person committed, detained, confined or restrained of his liberty, within this state, for any criminal or supposed criminal matter, or under any pretense whatsoever...may prosecute a writ of habeas corpus...to inquire into the cause of such confinement or restraint." "[A] writ of habeas corpus may be issued when a person is restrained of his or her liberty in violation of the constitution or

laws of the state or federal government." State ex rel. Amrine v. Roper, 102 S.W.3d 541, 545 (Mo. banc 2003). This court also has jurisdiction pursuant to Rule 91.02.

The Respondent asserts this case is moot because Mr. Oliver is no longer in prison or on parole and thus, he is no longer "retrained of his liberty." This assertion is false and does not conform with Missouri law. Petitioner was released on parole in 2007. The Petition for Writ of Habeas Corpus was filed on September 23, 2014, while the Petitioner was on parole with the Missouri Department of Probation and Parole. Petitioner was released from parole in 2018 2, while this case was awaiting trial.

While the Missouri Supreme Court has never interpreted the "restraint of his liberty" language, the Missouri Supreme Court has stated , when interpreting Missouri's habeas statute, that "any restraint which precludes freedom of action is sufficient and actual confinement in jail is not necessary." Hyde v. Nelson, 229 S.W. 200, 202 (Mo. 1921). The Missouri Supreme Court has twice reiterated the principle, that for the purpose of habeas relief, actual confinement is not necessary. See Nicholson v. State, 524 S.W.2d 106, 109 (Mo. banc 1975) ("[F]or purposes of habeas corpus, any restraint, which precludes freedom of action is sufficient, and actual

2 See Petitioner's Exhibit 2.

9

confinement is not necessary."); State v. Gray, 406 S.W.2d 580, 585 (Mo. 1966) ("[F]or purposes of habeas corpus, any restraint which precludes freedom of action is sufficient, and actual confinement in jail is not necessary."). Further, the Missouri Court of Appeals has held that it is appropriate for a parolee to seek habeas relief because he was restrained of his liberties. See State ex rel. Nixon v. Dierker, 22 S.W.3d 787, 789 (Mo. App. 2000) (holding that, because the parolee "was restrained of his liberty within this state and was inquiring into the cause of his restraint, a petition for a writ of habeas corpus was appropriate"). Additionally, section 217.690.2 states: "Every offender while on parole shall remain in the legal custody of the department [of corrections] but shall be subject to the orders of the board." The Missouri Supreme Court has held that a parolee was retrained of his liberties and could seek habeas relief pursuant to section 532.010 RSMo. See State ex rel. Fleming v. Missouri Board of Probation and Parole, 515 S.W.3d 224 (footnote 6, page 8) (Mo. 2017). Thus, the Petitioner, while on parole, was restrained of his liberties and was entitled to seek habeas relief pursuant to section 532.010 SMo.

Petitioner has since been released from parole. However, he is still entitled to seek habeas relief because the collateral consequences of his false conviction are restraints on his liberty, The United States Supreme Court has recognized that one need not be incarcerated or on probation or parole to seek habeas relief: "Clearly, the fact that petitioner is no longer in custody in any traditional sense does not automatically moot his claim for relief nor defeat federal jurisdiction over the matter." Carafas v. LaVallee, 391 U.S 234, 88 S.Ct. 1556, 20 L.Ed.2a 554 (1968). Carafas is like the case before the court in that Carafas was convicted in New York state court in 1960 and sought habeas relief in 1963. In 1967, while the habeas case was pending, his sentence expired, and he was released from parole. The , issue presented in Carafas was "whether the

10

expiration of petitioner's sentence, before his application was finally adjudicated and while it was awaiting appellate review, terminates federal jurisdiction with respect to the application." *Id* at 237. The Court held that it was "clear that petitioner's cause is not moot. In consequence of his conviction, he cannot engage in certain businesses; he cannot serve as an official of a labor union for a specified period; he cannot vote in any election held in New York State; he cannot serve as a juror. Because of these 'disabilities or burdens (which) may flow from' petitioner's conviction, he has 'a substantial stake in the judgment of conviction which survives the satisfaction of the sentence imposed on him. *Fiswick v. United States*, 329 U.S. 211, 222, 67 S.Ct. 224, 230, 91 L.Ed. 196 (1946). On account of these 'collateral consequences,' the case is not moot." *Id* at 237-38.

The United States Supreme Court, in another case, stated "[I]f there is any possibility that 'adverse collateral legal consequences' will flow from a prior conviction a defendant has sufficient stake in challenging that conviction to prevent the case becoming moot even though the defendant is no longer in custody or under parole." *Sibron v. State of New York*, 392 U.S. 40, 57-8, 88 S.Ct. 1889, 1899-1990, 20 L.Ed.2d 917 (1968).

As a result of the false conviction of murder in the first degree and assault in the first degree, the Petitioner has suffered collateral consequences beyond his 20-year incarceration. He was fired from jobs and not hired for jobs; he is unable to sit on a jury; he is unable to be a candidate for public office; he is forbidden to exercise his Second Amendment right to legally possess a firearm; and he faces housing restrictions. The Missouri Supreme Court in *Fleming v. Missouri Board of Probation and Parole*, 515 S.W.3d 224 (Mo., 2017) recognized that a parolee may seek habeas relief because being on parole is a restraint on the parolee's liberty. The United States Supreme Court has recognized that "adverse collateral legal consequences of a conviction is a sufficient stake to challenge a conviction to prevent the case from becoming moot even

11

hough the defendant is no longer in custody or under parole." Sibron v. State of
Iew York, 392 U.S. 40. Therefore, because the Petitioner sought habeas relief
vhile on parole and because of the "adverse collateral legal consequences" of his
alse conviction, the Petition for Writ of Habeas Corpus is not moot.

MANIFEST INJUSTICE

he Petitioner in this case is innocent of the crimes he was convicted of. The
Missouri
upreme Court has recognized that the prospect of the continued restraint and
onfinement of an innocent person is intolerable. State ex rel. Amrine v. Roper,
02 S.W.3d 541, 545 (Mo. Banc 2003). Prior to October 2016 people restrained of
heir liberty in Missouri could petition a court for a writ of habeas corpus under
he Actual Innocence Doctrine, which required that "evidence of actual innocence
nust be strong enough to undermine the basis for the conviction so as to make
he petitioner's continued incarceration...manifestly unjust even though the
onviction was otherwise the product of a fair trial." Id. at 547. The petitioner
ield the burden of producing clear and convincing evidence of actual innocence.
lowever in October 2016, while this Petition was pending, the Missouri Court of
appeals Western District issued Lincoln v. Cassady, 517 S.W.3d 11 (Mo.App.,
016) which held that "[u]ntil the [Missouri] Supreme Court announces that a
reestanding claim of actual innocence is a recognized basis for securing habeas
elief because either the continued incarceration or eventual execution of an
ctually innocent person violates
rinciples of due process, we have no authority to presume that Missouri's habeas
urisprudence permits such a claim in a non-death penalty case. Id. at 23. The
Missouri Supreme Court denied transfer of Lincoln to their docket in 2017 which
neans there is currently no free-standing claim of actual innocence in non-death
enalty cases in Missouri.
A .1. •••nnn••n

12

My case has never been about whether there is evidence of my guilt or innocence. My case has always been one excuse after another such as maybe a lawyer failed to do this or that—any loophole to not address the merits of my case was their approach. Mainly some way to blame me for someone else's fault. It is no different than trying to blame "white America" for doing something their great-great grandfather did years ago. We are to be accountable for ourselves and not responsible for everyone else. We were really feeling good about how things were coming together and how well my attorney was putting my argument together for my writ. We finally got a date to see the AAG and the judge, but the AAG after reading my brief began to start delaying this case. The first day that we met him he had my case mixed up with somebody else's case. My attorney told him that he needed to go back and study. AAG Gregory Goodwin said, "I think I'd better."

While we waited my attorney also asked the AAG to get the St. Louis, Missouri system to turn over the records and the files. They tried to claim that these records were 'privileged.' It took us over a year and then we still had to get the judge to call them on the phone to get the records. They even defied him for a while.

Missouri created a law called the Lincoln Case. It just so happened to come up while my writ of habeas corpus sat five years on the desk of Judge Daniel Green. In this law, Lincoln was serving a life without parole and was accused of killing a family member where the witness was I believe a young niece. When she grew up, she was watching a serial killer in the area on TV. It was then that she realized that he was the one who did the killing and not her uncle and she recanted her testimony. I don't know if this was the case or not, but Missouri adopted the Lincoln law to shut the door to actual innocent cases saying that unless you are a death row inmate, you do not have the right to claim actual innocence. This was an unlawful decree and it had nothing whatsoever to do with the injustice in my case. But, the 19th Circuit Court in Cole County chose to use this excuse to make my burden heavier than it ordinarily would have been. These are some of the illegal tactics Missouri uses to shut the door on innocent people from a proper and legal redress. The reason Lincoln came up is the Innocent Project was trying to get him off and it appears that Judge Daniel Green handled the case and we heard him say, "I don't know if I agree with this law." Up until then, actual innocence carried the day...whether a death row sentence or life without sentences. In other words, if you are innocent, you are not guilty and that does not take a rocket scientist to figure that out.

After the state denied my Writ of Habeas Corpus the state went on to break a federal law by creating mootness years after I filed for the state Writ of Habeas Corpus. My next step was to file a Federal Writ of Habeas Corpus, Pro Se and the Federal Court claimed that it did not have the jurisdiction to rule, although they acknowledged there were still collateral issues stemming from my 1987 conviction. Not only did they break laws to get my conviction, but they fraudulently concealed their activities by concocting a story. The following is how and why the concoction began and the manipulations and cover-ups to hide the truth.

How the Fraudulent Concealment began:
1.   The City of St. Louis' head prosecutor, George Peach, was angry because my granddad contacted him pretending to be Senator "Jett" Banks. Once he had Mr. Peach on the phone, he told him the truth and pleaded

for my brother and I to be treated with fairness because one of his grandsons was innocent and the other was mentally impaired. Mr. Peach responded by telling him, "Because you have done this thing, your grandsons will never see the light of day." i.e., see Prosecutor's deposition where he discussed his relationship with Mr. Peach his boss, which exposed the corruption in that office back then.

2.   The case was tried on a civil statute 491.074 relating to inconsistent statements against one of the state's own witnesses, Elizabeth. In 1987 it was illegal to use that statute in a criminal case because it allowed the prosecutor to impeach his own witness and gave overzealous prosecutors and police a chance to fabricate evidence.

   a.   The prosecutor built a case where both Ernest Fields and a couple of the police officers perjured themselves and said that Elizabeth told them that Ronald told her they were going to Lee and Fair to shoot the place up. Elizabeth emphatically denied that and, in the prosecutor's notes he wrote "EF (Ernest Fields) called and left a message saying, "Elizabeth said, "they were going to find Diane Moore," the second shooting victim. This is proof that the prosecutor allowed suborn perjury into this trial when the story that they were going there to shoot the place up came out of three witnesses. We did not receive these notes until 2019.

   b.   Elizabeth was the alleged kidnapped victim who swore she was not kidnapped.

   c.   Elizabeth was the only person who saw Ronald reload the gun without Gregory's presence. TV interview of Elizabeth's video, it too was accepted

202

into evidence. The trial judge injected in a 19-page memorandum defending the erroneous verdict that Gregory reloaded the gun instead of unloading it. He defended the jury selection, and he glorified the worst hearsay on hearsay witness Earnest Field who the prosecutor's notes now prove committed suborn perjury because he perjured himself by saying Ronald said "they" were going to Lee and Fair.... This is how they were trying to connect me to the shooting.

d. Elizabeth was the only one who could identify the relatives on the jury who were related to the witness at large Ernest Fields. (Elizabeth TV interview video)

e. Elizabeth was mentioned in the Prosecutors notes as being the mother of Ernest Fields's niece, confirming the prosecutor had knowledge of Elizabeth's knowledge of the Fields' family. She also knew that Ernest Fields was the brother-in-law of Bruce Campbell the deceased. This information was also in the prosecutor's notes, yet it did not come out at trial, which was another fact that was in the prosecutor's notes but at trial, he just built their relationship as friends through leading questions. The reason that the information about Elizabeth's relationship with the Field's family is critical because the use of 491.074 did not allow for a proper cross-examination of Elizabeth. Therefore, none of the critical information that she had came out at trial.

3. The Appellate Court also agreed that it was an error to use the statute 491.074, but considered it a harmless error, yet I do not know how much they were aware of

the fraudulent concealment that was going on to protect an erroneous verdict. Ten years later we found out that Judge Simeone the most assertive of the Appellate Court Judges was the mentor of the Trial Judge Robert Dierker. Although he saw the verdict was erroneous as stated at the appeal hearing, he chose to push for upholding the verdict.

4. My chief advocate, Bonnie was at the appeal hearing and witnessed Judge Simeone saying that "I didn't murder anyone, and it is also true that the critical issue in the case is why the court upheld the jury decision. Then the judge struck out Bonnie for writing the court and challenging the integrity of the lower court. He was so mad he even scared my lawyer who had given Bonnie both sides of the argument before the hearing that is why she was able to write the challenge the way she did. Six hours later Potosi Police arrested her while she was visiting me to share how the hearing went. She spent six hours in jail, three in the drunk tank waiting for the O'Fallon, MO Police to come and take her back to O'Fallon where she had lived four years prior. The charge "A dog off a leash" from when she lived in O'Fallon. After the arrest, she was issued a summons from an old neighbor complaint that had never been followed upon. She spent six hours in jail, was mug shotted and fingerprinted twice and was transported 125 miles handcuffed in the back of a police car for not even a misdemeanor. That is when she knew for sure that there was something fraudulent in my case or they would not have tried to shut her up.

5. The second 1st Degree Criminal Assault charge was dropped just before the trial began against Andrew Chambers. We believe so the prosecutor could hide his

own witness who had exculpatory evidence in his testimony to prove I had no part in Ronald's crazy shooting outburst. Come to find out the charge was dropped because the DEA put pressure on the prosecution because the victim was their highest-paid CI and was working the case at Diane Moore's house which was a drug house. The prosecutor's deposition mentions that he remembers the DEA was involved in this case. We have the redacted File on the CI Andrew Chambers proving that the DEA was known for protecting him and proves he was a documented liar when it came to who he was and what he was a party to.

6. In the prosecutor's deposition, he admitted that they had given Ronald Oliver, who actually did have a mental disease and defect, _a double dose of Mellaril_, an antipsychotic drug so he could be tried in front of a jury (the governor's office was able to get Ronald's _sealed_ medical records open to confirm Ronald's brain damage). We did not find out about the double dose until the prosecutor's deposition in 2019. The jury witnessed his blank stare and lethargic demeanor at the trial and the prosecutor kept drawing the jury's attention to it, which threw blame on me because I was cognizant and capable looking.

7. The bomb and arson squad went to the crime scene and there was no evidence of gasoline being splashed on the floor as witnesses testified that there was. At trial, the bomb and arson squad was not called to testify although other testimony said I was planning on burning the house down. Instead, the prosecutor used another policeman and with leading testimony, he agreed with the prosecutor that the odor, he smelled was gasoline, when it was the odor of PCP which smells like formaldehyde.

8. There were three police officers that the prosecutor used to perjure themselves to reinforce the concocted story that the court was trying to build.

9. Three plus years after the state Writ of Habeas Corpus petition was filed, my wife had to go to Michigan to take care of her mother and sister. I asked the Parole and Probation office if I could get a transfer up to Michigan. Once Michigan accepted my case, they also asked for all the paperwork so that they would know who they were dealing with. Before my very first appointment with my parole officer in Michigan, Missouri refused to turn over the File and immediately took me off papers. This clearly was another part of the fraudulent conceal-ment and the very thing they used to create the moot-ness issue. I only asked for a hardship transfer and my state writ was still in process the entire five years we waited for a decision. Notwithstanding, the AAG at the Hearing asked the Judge to put a protective order on the file he gave to my attorneys, so we couldn't go to the News media once we discovered the Governor's file at the hearing. It was the AAG that said he had to find something bad against me because he was not happy with the way the prosecutor, Garrett Randall's deposi-tion went in California.

10. The Governor's file was sent to our lawyers by the AAG. Once our lawyers read it they called the AAG and asked him to just give in because it was obvious that I was innocent. The AAG said he had to ask his boss first and when he got back with our lawyers, *he asked them to destroy the file because he was not supposed to give it to them*. Ah, fraudulent concealment! The Gov-ernor's investigation also exposed the damage this did to me by trying these cases together.

11. All the governor's investigation found pertaining to me was my innocence. The only thing that they could see that might be construed as a crime was that *__I MIGHT have been guilty of a misdemeanor that MIGHT have called for 1 year in jail/prison.__* Because they didn't charge me with that the statute of limitations would not have allowed them to go back over 20 years nor is their allowance giving me a 2nd-degree murder charge to commute my sentence. In the governor's notes, you will see that they tried to convince the governor this was not the remedy when he already stated that I was innocent. The remedy was a Full Pardon.

This is a brief overview of just some of the evidence. We have much more, i.e., Blood evidence, forensic evidence, sound evidence, and more.

CHAPTER 26
Final Thoughts
by
Gregory

My wife, Bonnie wrote a song that went along with the drawing she did that you see in this book and Bonnie's book *"Faithwalk A Walk from Darkness to the LIGHT"* entitled, "Walk A Mile in My Shoes." Her book is about her struggles becoming the vessel God called her to be as she battled unrelenting to fight for my freedom. The words to the song are:

Chorus
Walk a mile in my shoes, walk a mile in my shoes,
Walk a mile in my shoes you have nothing to lose.
Verse
Though the way is rugged
And the road is long.
Walk a mile in my shoes,
I will carry you along.
Chorus
Verse
I hear you crying out loud.
I know the pain in your heart.
Walk a mile in my shoes.
We will never part.

Chorus
Verse
Walk a mile in my shoes,
Walk a mile in my shoes,
Walk a mile in my shoes,
You have only to choose.

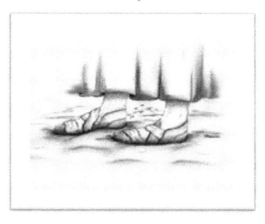

The final thought I want to leave with you is that we are all on a journey. In that journey sometimes there are valleys, mountain tops, seemingly defeats, triumphs, laughter, pain, and tears. But when we walk a mile in the Lord's shoes and pick up our cross. There is one thing to remember, we are going to go through much, but what I have learned is that the key is we are not stuck...we are going to go through. You know Bonnie's last name was Stuck when I met her, but she is no longer stuck in the rut of despair that she was in. God used her to do mighty works for him. Our news media picks up triumphant stories all the time some are and some are not, but what God was able to do through this woman, as courageous as she was, is beyond triumphant.

I remember a story about a man who did mighty works for the Lord in a foreign land and on his way back on a ship, there was a celebrity on board. As they got close to shore, he noticed there were crowds of people, a parade, balloons, bands to greet this celebrity and as he got off these people greeted him with hugs and love. The missionary that had served the Lord faithfully said to the Lord, "I have been faithful in my duties and have done mighty works for the Kingdom and I get home and there is not even one person to greet me."

The Lord simply told him, "That is because you are not home yet."

During the time I was in prison, Bonnie saved every gift she couldn't send to me inside. A friend of hers told her I would walk out of prison on a Monday. On Monday, June 11, 2007, I walked out of prison and Bonnie was waiting outside the door for me. First, we went to McDonald's so she could treat me to my first fast food in over 22 years. Then we drove to our friend's house, Fae who lived south of Jefferson City. I thank God for Fae even to this day her husband is still in prison. Yet she opened up her house for Bonnie to allow me to come there and surprise me with the many gifts she had awaiting me. What a person of selflessness. These are the type of people that God looks at and great rewards await them. I don't know how long it took for me to open the many gifts that were saved for me over the years, but it gave me a glimpse of heaven. When we get home, which is not in this earth, those that truly are going to be tremendously blessed. His Word says it best,

"*But as it is written, Eye hath not seen, nor ear heard, neither have entered into the heart of man, the things which God hath prepared for them that love him.* (1 Corinthians 2:9)

The woman that told Bonnie that I would be walking out of prison on a Monday also said that I would have some kind of a hearing and I WILL win my case. It was years later after I was out that I got to meet Joyce and her husband to thank her personally. I was heading to St. Louis and I had to pass through Chicago from Michigan so we met in the Chicago suburbs. We were trying to think of a place to meet. We finally decided to meet at Mackey D's. As I was telling her the testimony of how she had told Bonnie that I would walk out of prison on a Monday and that is exactly what happened. Suddenly, I told her Bonnie and I stopped at Mc Donald's the day I walked out. She quickly said, "We are at McDonald's now!" I knew no one could have orchestrated this but the Lord. We had a good visit and she and her husband are very special people. As the Lord is my witness, I AM "WALKING FREE"

CHAPTER 27

Government Heroes
By
Gregory & Bonnie

Throughout our fight against the State of Missouri, we ran into a lot of obstacles that were created by people not honoring the oath they swore to uphold the law. Through Gregory's trial and different levels of appeal, we wrestled with illegalities created by the few and seemingly covered up all the way up the ladder because they viewed everything in favor of the erroneous verdict. But...then...we had the pleasure of knowing four government heroes that we would like to honor with our books. *"Faithwalk: A Walk from Darkness to the Light"* by Bonnie Oliver and *"Walking Free: From Bondage to Liberty"* by Gregory Oliver. In both books, there is a special few who took their jobs seriously. They showed compassion and honored the law as the framers intended it to be honored. They also taught us that we needed to fight the law with the law and peel back the layers of bad law with good law like the skin of an onion.

The first hero that took up the gauntlet was Cranston Mitchell, Director of the Probation and Parole Office and Clemency Board. He was Bonnie's first glimmer of hope after spending two years fearful of the so-called good guys in the state of Missouri after she was thrown in jail on a trumped-up charge to try and back her off Gregory's case. Through the years he was the person Bonnie knew would be straightforward with her and he is the one whose words she drew upon during seasons when she wanted to give up. "Don't give up." He told her. He knew what was going on behind the scenes but couldn't reveal it. Time and time again his words ran through her mind whenever the road seemed too difficult to navigate. Gregory never met Mr. Mitchell personally, which was sad, he would have really liked him. Gregory knew, however, that he was the one who could initiate his request for Clemency.

Heroine number two was Shellie Freund a young attorney hired by the governor's office to study the clemency requests for approval or disapproval. Bonnie spent hours going over Greg's case with her and clarifying any questions that either of their studies might have generated. She never hesitated to let Bonnie know how the state would view things so that Bonnie would learn how to navigate through the opposition. She was studied and focused on the proper application of the law.

Hero number three was Joe Bednar, Chief Legal Counsel to Governor Mel Carnahan. When Bonnie first met Joe, they met in a poorly lit law library in the back of the governor's office. At their first meeting, Bonnie challenged him with her knowledge of Greg's case. He took the challenge. Through the years, he was open to whatever new information was presented to him no matter what form it was in. As the rapport grew there was an openness and respect that also grew between them.

Then there is the late Governor Mel Carnahan who was a lawyer himself and who honored the law and was not afraid to make a righteous judgment in lieu of negative feedback.

Gregory met both Joe Bednar and Shellie Freund at the prison. They wanted to get to know the person of Gregory seeing they were looking at pardoning him.

This legal team's integrity, responsiveness, and courage will remain in our hearts as being the kind of people that we wish everyone in government would be. They honored their oath and always sought to do what was right...not what is popular as so many of our politicians, government employees, and legislators base their values on.

Due to their zeal even though the incoming governor only commuted Gregory's sentence, that is the very thing that has given us the tenacity to carry on continuing to fight Gregory's case until his name is clear.

Gregory served this country and believed in the constitution as the framers wrote it. It was God who instructed him to study constitutional law to equip us for the fight. At each juncture of the fight, Greg's knowledge of the law is what ministered to Bonnie each step of the way. She was the face of the State of Missouri v. Gregory Oliver and needed his knowledge and his prayer covering.

After Gregory was released, Gregory had a chance to talk to twelve legislators in Jefferson City, MO. When he finished sharing, their response was, "Why did it take so long to get you out?"

The delay was because of the "Gordian Knot" of legal lies that surrounded my case could be the only answer.

If thou seest the oppression of the poor, and violent perverting of judgment and justice in a province, marvel not at the matter: for he that is higher than the highest regardeth; and there be higher than they.

Moreover, the profit of the earth is for all: the king himself is served by the field. (Ecclesiastes 5:8-9)